THE PRACTICE OF PRACTISING

ALESSANDRO CERVINO
CATHERINE LAWS (ed.)
MARIA LETTBERG
TÂNIA LISBOA

[ORCiM] 04

Leuven University Press

CONTENTS

Preface by Catherine Laws and Tânia Lisboa   5

I. A self-study of learning the Prelude from Bach's Suite No. 6 for cello solo: Comparing words and actions

—TÂNIA LISBOA, ROGER CHAFFIN, TOPHER LOGAN   9

    Prologue   9
    Effective practice   9
    The investigation   10
    Stages and cycles in learning the prelude   13
    Relating practice and reports   15
    Comparing practice and comments   17
    Stage 1: exploration   18
    Stages 2 and 3: smoothing out and listening   20
    Stage 4: re-working technique   22
    Stage 5: preparation for performance   24
    Connecting theory and practice   26
    Coda   29
    References   30
    Acknowledgements   31

II. Performer's harmony: towards a performance of Elliott Carter's Piano Sonata

—ALESSANDRO CERVINO   33

    Preliminary remarks   33
    Getting started   33
    The process   35
    The practice of practising: a tool for knowing   43
    Afterword   44
    References   47

III. Morton Feldman's Late Piano Music: Experimentalism in Practice

—CATHERINE LAWS   49

    Memory and subjectivity in Feldman's late music   51
    The problem of interpretation   53

Palais de Mari and the contingencies of performance	55
Practice as an experimental process	65
References	67

IV. Alfred Schnittke's Piano Trio: Learning and Performing
— MARIA LETTBERG

	69
Introduction	69
Preparation for rehearsals and recording	71
Achieving affinity	79
Conclusions	84
References	87

Personalia 89

PREFACE
CATHERINE LAWS AND TÂNIA LISBOA

The processes of practising are intrinsic to musical creativity. Practice is exploratory, and can encompass aspects of interpretation, improvisation and even composition. Moreover, the boundaries between the technical and the musical in practising are often inseparable. Performers strive for high levels of technical control in order to express musical creativity.

To date, however, the literature on practice has been primarily pedagogical, concerned with suggestions for practice routines and methods, focusing on 'effective' practice and how to get the 'best' results from practice time. Similarly, music psychology has scrutinised the content of performers' practice regimes, at times assessing the relationship to acts of performance. As a result, in both conventional research contexts and the emerging field of artistic research, scant attention has been paid to the significance of practice, and especially to the role of embodied experience—of understanding gained through *doing*—in the forming of musical ideas.

Certainly, the practice of expert musicians has been a rich source of information and data for psychologists, analysts, and musicologists. Existing research has relied heavily on observation and retrospective interviewing. However, discussions between Artistic Research Fellows at the Orpheus Research Centre in Music (ORCiM) in Ghent revealed a desire for a volume written by performer-researchers themselves. Out of this was born this collection of four essays, all rooted in practice-led research that includes self-reflection as a valuable and distinctive contribution. The volume comprises four diverse case studies of individual practice in relation to music by J. S. Bach, Elliott Carter, Morton Feldman and Alfred Schnittke, incorporating a range of approaches in preparing for performance: from solo to ensemble playing, from memorising to performing, from the stage to the recording studio.

The Practice of Practising is, therefore, a volume that focuses precisely on the strategies, methods and concepts of practising. It explores various processes in developing technical and musical ideas and in preparing for both performance and recording situations. In doing so, it aims to convey some of the creative content of the authors' practices. The reader is invited into the practice room, the space in which the performer explores a field of artistic possibilities. It is a place to experiment, to generate and refine ideas, to try things differently: a private and playful space, in contrast to the decisive moment of exposure to the ears of the public. Ultimately, then, *The Practice of Practising* includes reflections that contribute to more established approaches; but it is primarily concerned with moving beyond, into the consideration of practising as a *practice in itself*—a collection of processes that determines musical creativity and significance.

The first chapter describes Tânia Lisboa's collaboration with two specialists in music psychology, Roger Chaffin and Topher Logan: a project designed to gain a better understanding of the processes of learning, memorising and performing the Prelude from J.S. Bach's Suite No. 6 for cello solo. Expert learning in music is compared to theories of expert problem solving in other fields, and the authors examine the relationship between the musician's conceptualisation of the process—as evidenced in her detailed logbooks and recorded commentary—and her practice. As a result, Lisboa is able to reflect not only on the technical and creative impact of her practice as a whole but also on the influence of this kind of self-reflective scrutiny in relation to her extensive performance experience.

Alessandro Cervino's focus is somewhat different, oriented towards the ways in which his practice led to a particular understanding of Elliott Carter's Piano Sonata (1945-6, revised 1982)—one that, he argues, could not have been achieved away from the instrument. While the focal point is the performer's approach to Carter's harmony, Cervino's discussion of his process highlights the interdependency of aspects of melody, harmony, rhythm, and articulation (including piano touch and tone and the use of the pedal). Ultimately, Cervino demonstrates the significance of the embodied experience at the instrument in the different perceptions of form and structure that arise from minor changes to the articulations of the various musical parameters. As a result, he argues for the value of reflecting on the practice of practising as a tool for greater musical understanding.

For the third chapter we stay with the piano, but in contrast to Cervino, Catherine Laws's chapter is concerned with a degree of unknowability. Focusing on the late piano music of American experimental composer Morton Feldman, Laws argues against practice as means of establishing an intentional musical interpretation and thereby minimising the uncertainties inherent to performance. Instead, Laws examines the ways in which Feldman's music opens one to a practice alert to the uncertainties and contingencies of instrumental performance—to its very performativity.

Finally, in the fourth chapter, Maria Lettberg takes us into the world of chamber music, and away from the concert hall into the recording studio. She takes as a case study her individual practice and subsequent ensemble rehearsals for a recording of Alfred Schnittke's Piano Trio (1992), demonstrating the function of particular score mapping systems designed to aid practice in the solo and group contexts. Lettberg is concerned to present the 'inside' view, examining her own perceptions of the processes and their practices. Beyond this, her discussion articulates the ways in which the performers' individual musical responses to the instrumental material is in part conditioned by contextual understanding, in this case the composer's polystylistic approach and his use of musical allusion.

Each chapter offers contextualised insights with regard to specific practices but also moves beyond its particular repertoire, tackling more broadly relevant issues and paying attention to the relationships and divergences between embodied and verbalised knowledge, intention and action, and the habitualised and the unpredictable. Together, the chapters articulate ways in which insight is gained and transformed through the action of practice, how the process of practising can generate self-reflective awareness of its very practices—a kind of meta-practice, perhaps, but one that is entirely predicated on embodied experience.

ACKNOWLEDGEMENTS

We would like to thank all contributors to this book, in particular Roger Chaffin and Topher Logan. Thanks, also, to our colleagues at ORCiM for their support.

I.
A self-study of learning the Prelude from Bach's Suite No. 6 for cello solo: Comparing words and actions

TÂNIA LISBOA, ROGER CHAFFIN, TOPHER LOGAN

PROLOGUE

What are the strategies, thoughts and artistic behaviours involved in learning a new piece? We answer these questions by describing how an experienced cellist prepared for performance the Prelude from Bach's Suite No. 6, for cello solo, BWV 1012. The chapter describes my (the first author's) experience and insights as a musician studying my own practice with the help of collaborators: psychologists who study music cognition. The longitudinal case study described here took place over a period of 3½ years during which we recorded the process of learning, memorising and giving ten public performances of the Prelude—a total of 38 hours of practice in 75 practice sessions.

EFFECTIVE PRACTICE

Musicians have been interested in methods for effective practice for many years, at least since Carl Czerny's famous report of his lessons with Ludwig van Beethoven (Czerny 1970) and Leopold Mozart's treatise on the fundamental principles of violin playing. Recently, Anders Ericsson and colleagues have provided empirical evidence for the importance of effective practice. Even among exceptional performers, the level of achievement is closely related to the amount of *deliberate* practice. A minimum of ten years and 10,000 hours of deliberate practice are required to achieve eminence (Ericsson, Krampe and Tesch-Römer 1993; Ericsson 1997). Given the number of hours involved, even small differences in the effectiveness of practice may be important (Chaffin and Lemieux 2004).

One simple way to identify effective methods of music practice empirically is to interview eminent performers (e.g., Hallam 1995, 1997; Chaffin, Imreh and Crawford 2002, 26–65). Nevertheless, despite their interest, interviews are of limited value due to the possibility of inaccuracy and distortion (Ericsson and Simon 1980). Experiments have the advantage of objectivity and can also assess the efficacy of different practice techniques (e.g., Rubin-Rabson 1941). Experiments, however, are limited by the need to study practice techniques that have already been identified, and by the possibility that the artificial tasks involved may overshadow the creative problem-solving that is of interest. Naturalistic observation of practice provides a happy compromise, combining objectivity with ecological validity (e.g., Gruson 1988; Miklasewski 1989; Nielsen 1999; Williamon, Valentine and Valentine 2002). One variant is to enlist the cooperation of the artist in a longitudinal case study in which the musician studied also becomes a full member of the research team (e.g., Chaffin, Imreh and Crawford 2002; Ginsborg, Chaffin and Nicholson 2006). This was our approach.

The prospect of studying one's *own* practice, however, can be terrifying. Might scrutinising the process destroy the 'spell' or compromise the 'freshness' of performance? I confronted such fears repeatedly during the course of our study. The process was challenging, and my dual roles as performer and investigator had to be carefully managed. In the end, the combination of self-reflection and the gaining of objective information about what actually happened during practice led to a positive outcome. I gained a deeper understanding of the music and of my own practice. As a result, my learning has become more focused and memorising has become easier, quicker and more reliable.

THE INVESTIGATION

As I started practising, I restrained myself from reading reports of other studies by my collaborators so as to avoid influencing my usual practice behaviour. However, towards the end of the learning process, as I became more involved in the analysis and interpretation of the data, I took a more active role as a researcher. I began to read my colleagues' previous publications so that together we could understand how the data we were collecting related to psychological theories of memory, expertise, and skill acquisition. Sometimes the match of theory to data was straightforward, but often elaboration was needed. My experience as a musician and my understanding of my own musical goals for the Prelude were critical in mapping the abstract constructs of psychological theory onto the messy reality of my long hours in the practice studio.

I kept a log book in which I recorded notes about each practice session. As I practised, I spoke periodically to the camera, commenting on my playing, goals, progress, strategies, frustrations, and much else. My psychologist colleagues transcribed my comments and also where I started and stopped in my practice. We then classified the comments into the six categories shown in table 1.[1]

Category	Topics
Technique	Bowing; Fingering; Hand Position; Change of Strings; Intonation; Vibrato
Musical Structure	Formal Structure; Harmonic Structure; Melodic Structure
Interpretive	Articulation; Dynamics; Phrasing
Memory	Conceptual Memory; Difficulty; Memory Cue
Metacognitive	Concentration; Evaluation; Stages
Strategies	Counting; Practice Tempo; Rhythmic Variations, etc.

Table 1. Categories used to classify comments made during practice, with examples of topics.

My colleagues also provided me with graphs of my practice sessions showing where I started and stopped. The graphs showed fascinating patterns of activity: bouts of focused work intermittently connected together into longer runs. To improve understanding of what was going on, I provided reports about every aspect of my musical thinking during practice. Around session 33, I marked the musical structure and all of my decisions about technique and interpretation on copies of the score. Later, around session 68, I reported my *performance cues* (PCs) in the same way. PCs are those aspects of the piece to which I paid attention during performance; the landmarks in my mental map of the piece that told me where I was and what came next (see Chaffin, Lisboa, Logan and Begosh 2010).

We used these retrospective reports to gain a better understanding of what I was doing during my practice sessions. By the time I saw the graphs, many months had passed and I no longer had detailed memories of individual practice sessions. By comparing the practice graphs with my reports, we were able to identify the aspects of the music to which I was paying attention during practice.

---

1 An additional category of 'other' comments, mainly directed at my colleagues to assist with transcription (such as the bar numbers of my starting points), is excluded from this description.

For example, if I started repeatedly at beginnings of sections, then we inferred that I was thinking about the musical structure. If I started repeatedly at places where I reported decisions about dynamics, then we inferred that I was thinking about dynamics. We have described these analyses in an earlier report of this study (Chaffin et al. 2010). Here, we will draw on the earlier report to compare what I *did* in practice with what I *said*.

The contrast between practice and comments is striking. They provide different windows into a musician's mind (Chaffin and Imreh 2001). I talked about the problems that preoccupied me—for example, the technical issues about fingering and bowing that the Prelude presents because it was written for a five-stringed instrument rather than for the four-stringed contemporary cello. These problems were also reflected in my practice, of course. But practice was also affected by other aspects of the music that I thought about more fleetingly and less explicitly—more intuitive aspects of playing—and by habits deeply ingrained over time. For example, I spoke very little about the musical structure but, as we will see, it provided the framework for my practice. My practice was also influenced by thoughts that were more ineffable, feelings about expressive goals that were hard to articulate. These intuitions shaped my music-making directly, without the intervention of words. Subsequent reflection on the relationship between comments and practice has provided me with a new understanding of how these different aspects of musical creativity shape my activities as a musician.

Tânia Lisboa, Roger Chaffin, Topher Logan

STAGES AND CYCLES IN LEARNING THE PRELUDE

My practice moved through stages similar to those identified in previous research (Wicinski 1950, reported in Miklaszewski 1989). However, I initially found it quite difficult to identify and label such stages. For instance, while I was still in the middle of learning the Prelude and had to prepare our first conference report on this project, I noted that "[I] found it impossible to reduce the detailed and complex memory of [my] progress to a set of tidy stages and boxes" (Lisboa, Chaffin, Schiaroli and Barrera 2004). A year later, after examining the practice graphs, I was able to identify a clear progression in my work on the piece, and it was at this point that I divided my learning into the following five stages: *exploring the piece, smoothing out, listening, reworking technique*, and *preparing for performance*. I needed the distance in time, as well as the objective record of my practice, to recognise the larger-scale patterns. Table 2 lists the number and duration of the practice sessions in each stage and provides a timeline, showing where I took long breaks from my work on the Prelude (while preparing other repertoire; see Chaffin et al. 2010).

Learning Period	Initial Learning				First Re-Learning				Second Re-Learning
Stage (goal)	Exploration	Smoothing Out	Listen	B R E A K	Rework Technique	Prepare Performance		B R E A K	Prepare Performance
Practice sessions	1-10	11-19	20-32		33-35	36-47	48-67		68-75
Duration (hrs:min)	5:58	7:10	4:34		2:24	5:12	8:04		4:17
Duration (weeks)	3	6	3		1	5	1		4
Public Performances						1-2	3-8		9-10

Table 2. Overview of the learning process, showing the main breaks that divided learning into three periods, the five main stages, and the practice sessions in each stage, with duration of practice (number of hours practiced and weeks covered) for each stage, and when public performances took place.

THE PRACTICE OF PRACTISING

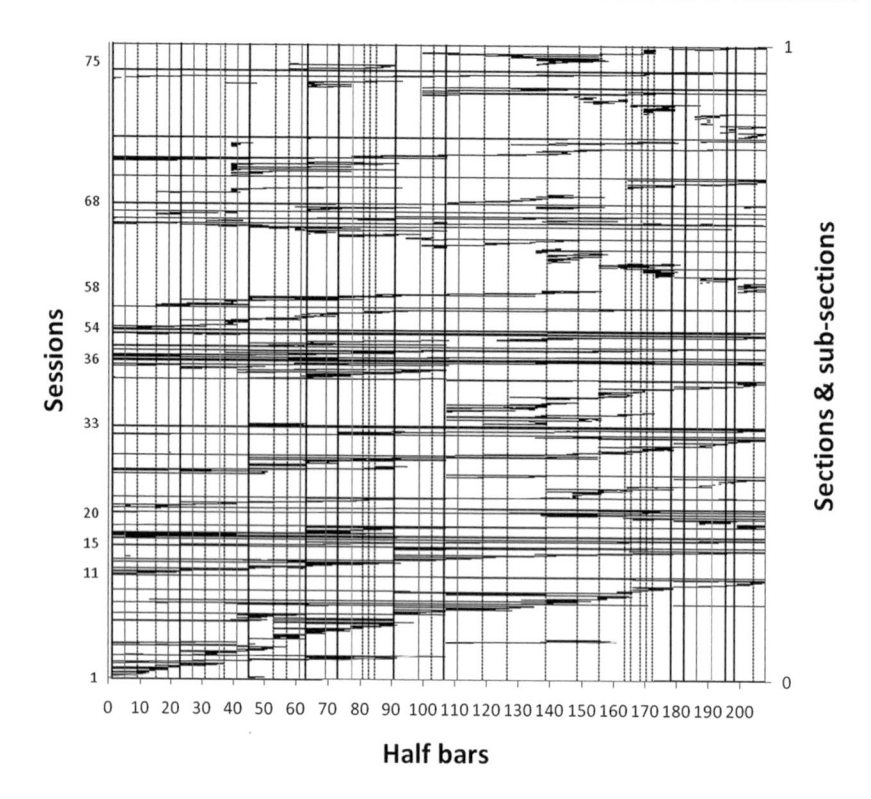

Figure 1. Practice graph of sessions 1–75 with vertical lines marking the locations of sections (dark lines) and sub-sections (paler lines).

Figure 1 shows the entire record of practice for sessions 1-75.[2] The graph reads from bottom to top with horizontal lines representing practice *segments*: uninterrupted playing. The horizontal axis represents the music, in half bars.[3] The vertical axis represents successive practice sessions, beginning with session 1 at the bottom and ending with session 75 at the top. Also numbered along this axis is the first session of each of the stages identified in table 2 and sessions 15 and 28, which are discussed in detail below. Also included are sessions 33 and 36,

---

2 The practice shown in figure 1 represents 59 of the 75 practice sessions and nearly 33 hours of the 38¼ hours of practice. Sessions 48 to 53 (approximately 2½ hours) following the first public performance were not video-recorded in order to see whether practicing without the distraction of the camera would make a difference. There is no reason to think these sessions were different from sessions that were recorded. Also not recorded were other sessions involving mental review of the piece before public performances and sessions that involved simply playing through the piece in a practice performance. These sessions were, however, recorded in the log book and are included in the total practice time.

3 We used half bars as the unit of analysis for the 12/8 time signature because it reflected the way in which I understood bar structure. See bars 3 and 4 for an example of half-bar repetition.

in order to delineate sessions 33-35, which are also discussed below. Within each session, successive practice segments read from bottom to top.

Inspection of figure 1 shows that practice cycled between *section-by-section* practice, in which I focused on individual sections of the Prelude, and *integrative* practice, in which my goal was to connect the various sections into a unified and coherent performance (Chaffin et al. 2010). This kind of alternating pattern within a session has been referred to as *work* and *runs* (Chaffin et al. 2002, 116-126). The pattern has been noted in several studies of expert music practice (Miklasewski 1989; Williamon et al. 2002). Our study is the first to observe the same pattern on a larger time scale, across practice sessions. Student musicians, in contrast to experts, are more likely to simply play through the piece (Lisboa 2008).

RELATING PRACTICE AND REPORTS

The vertical lines in figure 1 represent my reporting of the beginnings of main sections and sub-sections. Inspection shows that I often started and stopped at these locations. The intersections of horizontal lines, representing practice, and vertical lines, representing my reports, show that I used the formal structure of the music as a framework for practice. This is another characteristic of expert practice (Chaffin et al. 2002; Williamon et al. 2002).

I reported on every aspect of the music thought about during practice: bowing, fingering, technical difficulties, dynamics, intonation, and phrasing, along with performance cues for each (see Chaffin et al. 2010, table 1). Using practice graphs such as figure 1, we were able to see when each of these different aspects of the music related to the way in which I practised. For each report we asked the same question: did I start, stop, or repeat these places in the music more than others?

We used the statistical technique of multiple regression to simultaneously relate each of the different reports to the number of starts, stops, and repeats. Table 3 summarises the results, showing when each of fifteen types of report related to starts, stops, or repetitions. The top two rows of data in table 3 show that I used the beginnings of sections and subsections as starting and stopping places throughout most of the learning process. The statistical analyses thus confirm the conclusion already reached from visual inspection of figure 1: I used the musical structure as a framework for my practice.

Stage	Explore	Smooth	Listen	Re-work	Prepare Performance
Sessions	1-10	11-19	20-32	33-35	36-75
Structural Cues					
Expressive/Sections	B	BE	BE	B	B
Subsections	BE	BE	B		BE
Switches	E		E		
Performance Cues					
Interpretive				***BER***	***BER***
Intonation				ER	ER
Basic: left hand		ER	ER	E	***BER***
Basic: right hand			***BER***		-E
Interpretation					
Dynamics	***BER***				-R
Sound quality	R	R		R	***BER***
Intonation	R	-E	ER		***BER***
Phrasing		BR			B
Basic Technique					
Hand position	R	R	R		R
Fingering					
Bowing/Change string		E	ER		E
Technical difficulties			ER		***BER***

Table 3. Summary of effects (p<.01) on practice at each stage of learning. Effects on starts (B), stops (E) and repetitions (R) are shown separately for different types of performance cues and for each type of decision about interpretation and basic technique. Intensive practice (simultaneous effects on starts, stops and repetitions) is shown in **bold italics** (condensed from Chaffin et al. 2010, table 2).

Intensive practice (multiple repetitions of the same short passage), shown in bold italics in table 3, indicates that I was focusing on a particular problem, starting, stopping and repeating. In figure 1, intensive practice is represented by the small blocks of black ink that show where I repeated the same passage over and over, starting and stopping at the same place. Table 3 tells us when the various aspects of the music that I provided reports about received this kind of intensive treatment.

The distribution of intensive treatment suggests that my practice was guided more by my musical conception of the piece than by its technical challenges (Chaffin, Imreh, Lemieux and Chen 2003). Intensive practice in the initial, exploratory stage was directed at dynamics, as I established the building blocks of my interpretation. Intensive practice of technique does not appear until the final stage, preparing performance. I felt it was important to acquire a general musical conception of the piece before investing the time necessary to master the technique to project my musical ideas. In the next section, however, we will see that my comments suggest exactly the opposite strategy.

Tânia Lisboa, Roger Chaffin, Topher Logan

COMPARING PRACTICE AND COMMENTS

Figure 2 shows the proportion of comments (by category) for each of the five stages of the learning process. Inspection shows that I initially spoke a lot about technique and very little about interpretation. Across the five stages, the proportion of comments on technique decreased steadily, and the proportion on interpretation increased. The pattern makes sense: first technique, then interpretation. However, this is the opposite of the pattern for practice identified in table 2.

We have already discussed why practice and commentary might differ. In the early sessions my comments were mostly about technique, because I needed to make basic fingering and bowing decisions prior to playing the piece with fluency. However, I was not ready to do the extended work needed to secure technique until I was sure that it would work musically. Meanwhile, my playing was shaped by musical intuitions which I spoke less about, both because they were less problematic and also because they were hard to articulate. Later, as I started to think about projecting musical ideas, I talked more about interpretation. By this time, I had settled on the technical decisions and spoke about them less (though comments on technique were still in evidence, because I continued to work on it and also because these things are easy to talk about). Thus, practice and commentary both reveal my concerns, but in different ways and at different times.

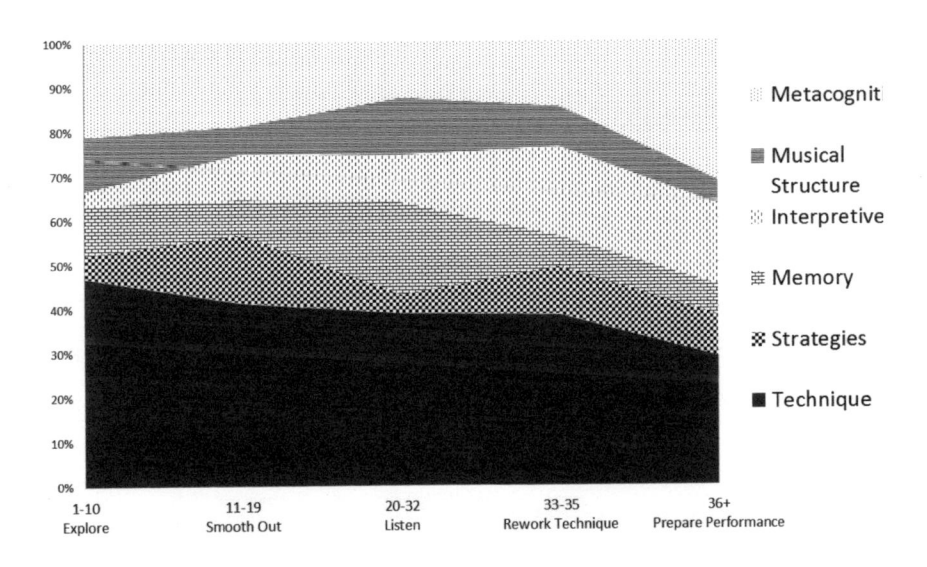

Figure 2. Proportion of the different categories of comments in each of five stages of learning.

STAGE 1: EXPLORATION

Practice

The practice record for session 1 is shown in figure 3. As in figure 1, each line represents the uninterrupted playing of a practice segment. At the bottom of the figure is my initial sight-reading through the entire piece. Although my playing was interrupted by technical difficulties and pitch mistakes, I tried to maintain the musical direction, focusing on the musical 'big picture' (i.e. an overall musical conception) rather than details of pitch, bowing and fingering. This first run-through gave me a sense of the overall musical shape and revealed the main technical problems. This was followed by the start of the section-by-section practice that would continue throughout the exploring stage. In session 1, I first looked briefly at the technical issues in half-bars 46–54, a passage that required many decisions about bowing and fingering. I then spent the rest of the session on the first section of the piece, half-bars 1–22.

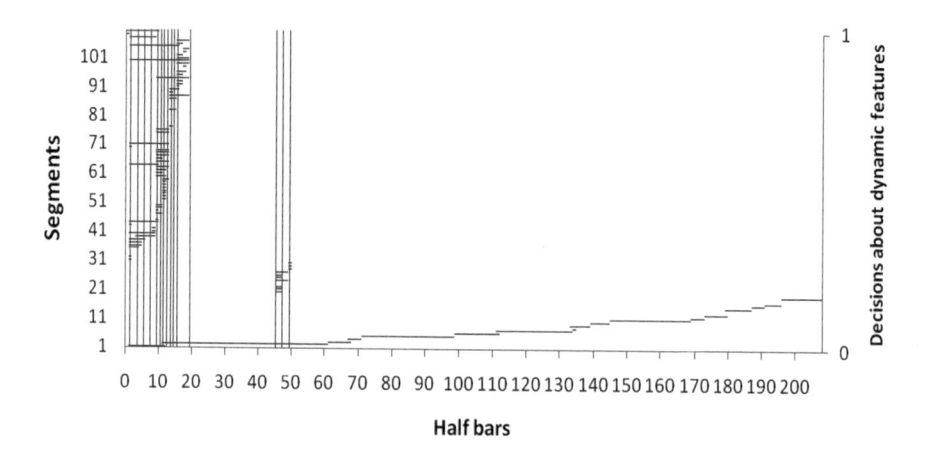

Figure 3. Practice graph for session 1, showing initial sight-reading through the piece at the bottom, followed by work on half-bars 46–52 and 1–22. The location of decisions about dynamics in worked-on passages is marked by vertical lines.

The vertical lines in figure 3 show the points of decision-making about dynamics. As mentioned above, I practised dynamics intensively in the initial exploratory stage. The intensive practice of dynamics is reflected in the intersections of the vertical lines (representing decisions about dynamics) with the beginnings and ends of horizontal lines (representing practice). Since Bach provided no dynamic markings (other than in the first two bars), this was simply my first reaction to the piece, using dynamic contrast to emphasise the implicit musical shape.

Comments

As already noted, the highest percentage of comments in sessions 1–10 concerned technique. I was acutely aware of the choices that I had to make with regard to fingering and bowing, and I talked about them even though I was not ready to make the final decisions. A typical comment from session 1 was: "I've got an option of fingering on bars 23 onwards to about bar 32, so I'm going to try a different fingering." Later, in session 3, I explained my strategy: "I'm looking at two different editions to check bowing to try and decide what to use. ... I'm going to follow the fingering from one edition, the bowing from the other one. ... One edition is technically more comfortable than the other, but I'm not sure if it works musically."

In session 3, I reached an important decision: "Okay, there's no way out. I have to decide musically what I want and then I can choose a fingering." In the end, I used the strategy I had described in session 3. However, I was not yet sure that this was going to work musically, and so I postponed work on the technical issues until much later. This is why there was no intense practice of technical difficulties, but plenty of comments about them, during these early practice sessions.

Instead, my practice was organised by the musical structure and the intensive practice of dynamics, which I scarcely mentioned. There was not a single comment about musical structure in session 1, and I mentioned dynamics only twice: "First bar forte, second bar piano. [The] repetition is the same."; and "I was just checking the ... dynamics ..."

STAGES 2 AND 3: SMOOTHING OUT AND LISTENING

Practice

Session 15 was a pivotal session: the first session of integrative practice and the first practice performance from memory. The integrative nature of the session is evident in the practice graph for session 15, in figure 4. I worked through the piece in short sections, using the musical structure to organise my practice as in previous sessions.[4] At the end of the session, I integrated the separate sections by playing through the entire piece. The practice performance appears as a single, unbroken line running across the top of figure 4. Before starting to play, I commented: "I'm going to keep the music here, but see if I can remember most of it. If I can't, I'll just look." As I finished: "Ok, I just about know it. I think it's memorised." I had played from memory.

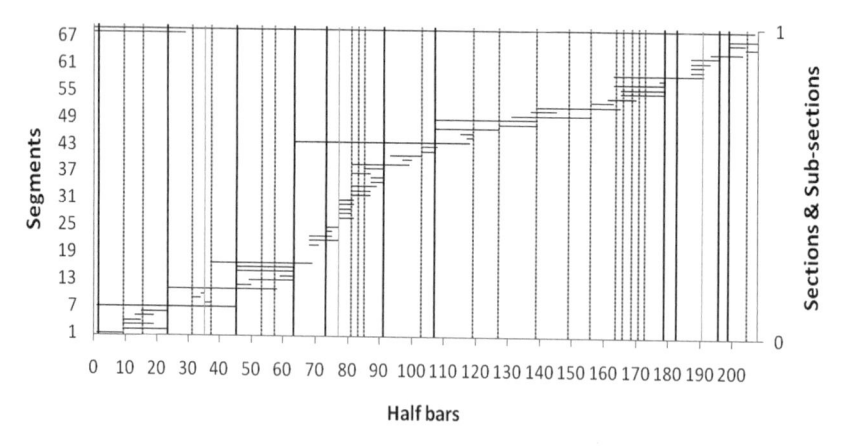

Figure 4. Practice graph for session 15, showing beginnings of sections (dark lines) and subsections (pale lines).

Comments

Session 15 is another example of the mismatch between my words and actions. I began the session by announcing, "I am not going to focus on memorisation. It's cold so I'm going to play slowly and concentrate on projection of sound

---

4   The report of musical structure identified five levels, hierarchically organised. Figure 4 shows the top level (sections) and two levels of subsections (top and bottom).

and getting the bow to speak clearly, and to work on left hand. It will be boring musically." Instead, for the first time, I talked extensively about interpretation and barely mentioned memorisation: "I've got a *diminuendo* in bar 7. ... Now ... it makes more sense. Do it one more time. ... See if I can do the *crescendo* in steps. ... From the beginning, thinking about accents ...". This is in complete contrast to preceding sessions in which I rarely mentioned interpretation but talked a lot about memorisation.

In the context of my comments, the decision at the end of the session to "see if I can remember most of it" seems sudden and unplanned. The practice graph, however, shows otherwise. I had spent the entire practice session systematically working through the piece, getting ready to put it together. In the context of my actions, my announcement at the outset—"I am not going to focus on memorisation"—takes on a different meaning: I would let memorisation take care of itself. I was announcing my memorisation strategy for the session.

'Smoothing out' continued with section-by-section work on technique in sessions 17–19. At the end of session 19, I reported: "I feel I am ready to move on ... I know the notes, bowing and fingering ... I need to think about phrasing [and] harmonies [to] bring them out. ... It is getting to the stage where I feel like I would very much like to listen to a recording of this by somebody. See how it compares to my understanding ...". This announced a change in focus that would characterise the listening stage.

During the listening stage, I continued to talk about interpretation but often linked it to other issues. For example, connections were made to: musical structure ("I've got two voices going on here"); technique ("the fingers are too articulated. [It] has to be smoother"); expression ("I'm going to ... get the whole [picture of the] phrasing, then try to do a bit more [with it] music[ally]"); practice strategy ("okay, I'll have to do a lot of listening ... for intonation"); and metacognition ("okay, I will try putting it all together"). At this stage, I listened to a variety of performances by other cellists, including Casals, Tortelier, and Fournier. I also watched the recordings of my own playing. The video recordings of my practice sessions provided me with an unusual opportunity to reflect on my own stage presence, posture, bodily movement, and degrees of relaxation.

Towards the end of the listening stage, I used a rehearsal at the Wigmore Hall in London to try the Prelude in the acoustics of a good concert hall. At the start of the next practice session I recorded my impression:

The acoustics are beautiful for the cello. I really enjoyed playing there. ... I was just basically trying to play through the music. ... It felt really wonderful and also gave me the feeling that this is starting to move towards a proper public performance in terms of thinking bigger ... [about] the projection of sound—the quality of sound; and of course that has technical implications for what I am trying to do.

STAGE 4: RE-WORKING TECHNIQUE

By this point, I knew how I wanted the piece to sound and now needed to ensure technical accuracy in order to project my musical ideas clearly. I made the necessary adjustments to my playing in sessions 33–35. Here, the focus of my practice changed to polishing technique, and so I identified this as a separate stage even though, at 3½ hours, it was much shorter than other stages. I wanted a clear sound, good intonation and well-projected phrasing, and I therefore needed to be accurate with hand positions, fingerings and bowings.

Practice

The practice for the entire re-working stage is shown in figure 5. The section boundaries here make it clear that I was still practising in sections. Unlike the integrative practice in session 15, however, I did not work through the whole piece in the same session, or attempt a practice performance. These sessions formed the final episode of section-by-section practice.

According to the analysis summarised in table 3, I engaged in intensive practice of interpretive PCs during this stage. In figure 5 we can see examples of this, where my playing started repeatedly at interpretive PCs. For example, the PCs in half-bars 135 and 139 were a repeated focus of attention in sessions 33 and 34 and again at the end of session 35, when an otherwise continuous run to the end of the piece was interrupted at these same places.[5] We see here how my interpretive PCs were established. Thinking about interpretive goals as I played

---

5 Two interpretive PCs at half bars 73 and 183 are not visible in figure 5 because they coincide with a section boundary.

a passage created a link between thought and action that could later guide my performance on stage.

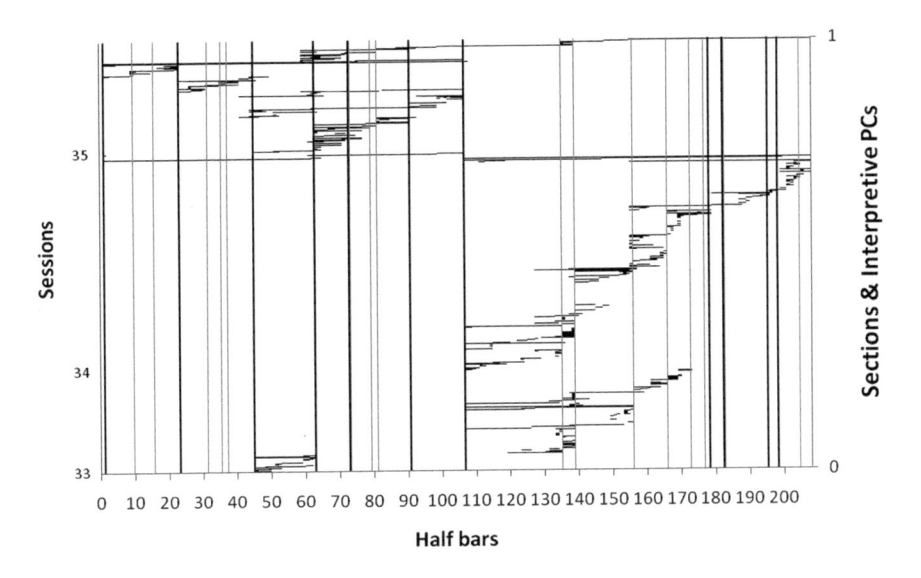

Figure 5. Practice graph for the 're-working stage' (sessions 33–35) showing beginnings of sections (dark lines) and interpretive performance cues (PCs; pale lines).

Comments

Here, for the first time, comments and practice tell the same story as to why I needed a performance cue in half-bar 135. I was having trouble with memory, confusing this passage with an earlier, similar passage. In session 33, I wondered, "Maybe [thinking about] the dynamics would help because I've got a *crescendo* on the up-bow ... and then one on the down bow." In session 34, I returned to the same point: "Okay, back to [half-bar 108], thinking about dynamics and articulation and phrasing." Figure 5 shows that I practised this PC repeatedly, starting at half-bar 108 and playing through to the PCs in half-bars 135 and 139 (see Chaffin et al. 2010).

At this point in the process, my comments focused more on interpretation than in earlier stages (see figure 2). In particular, I often spoke of musical goals: "Okay, um, I'm not doing the dynamics exactly where I should be"; "I have to play ... smoother, without too many accents"; "now it's dynamics, expression and everything." As in earlier sessions, I continued to voice my thoughts on technique, for example commenting, "I think I'll practise the new fingering for a bit longer and see if I can get used to it."

STAGE 5: PREPARATION FOR PERFORMANCE

More than a month before the first public performance—an informal house concert—my practice became more intense, marking a new stage of *preparation for performance*. Three more public performances followed the first in short order, and I then flew to the United States for a two-week stay with my collaborators, during which I was scheduled to give four additional performances.

Practice

Figure 6 shows the first practice session after my arrival in the United States. At 96 minutes, session 58 was much longer than any previous practice session. I described my plan at the beginning of the session:

> I'm going to start at the end, and I'm really going to concentrate on my left hand positions and intonation. I'm going to practise for quite a long time very slowly and sometimes just the bow ... for technique and security.

The section boundaries in figure 6 show that, although working backwards, I was still working in sections. The session provides another example of integrative practice; I worked through the entire piece, and concluded the session with a practice performance.

Perhaps the most striking change in my practice during this stage was the number of different aspects that were subject to intensive practice. In table 3, bold italics identify five sets of effects indicating that five different aspects of the music received this kind of treatment. Figure 6 shows three of these effects: PCs for interpretation (top panel), PCs for left hand (i.e. fingering: middle panel), and places where there were technical difficulties (bottom panel). In addition, table 3 shows intensive practice of sound quality and intonation in this stage; these are not shown in figure 6.

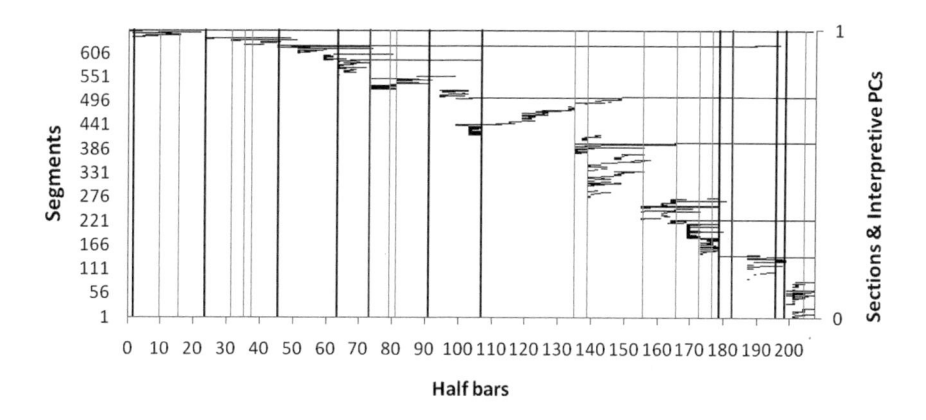

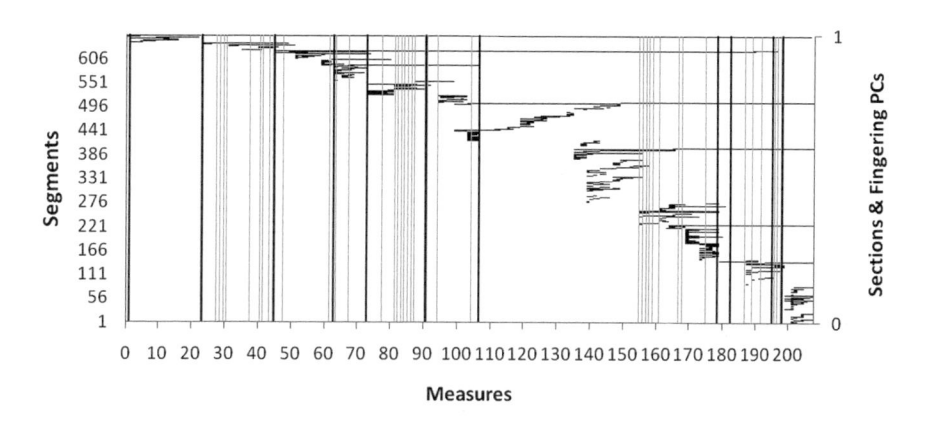

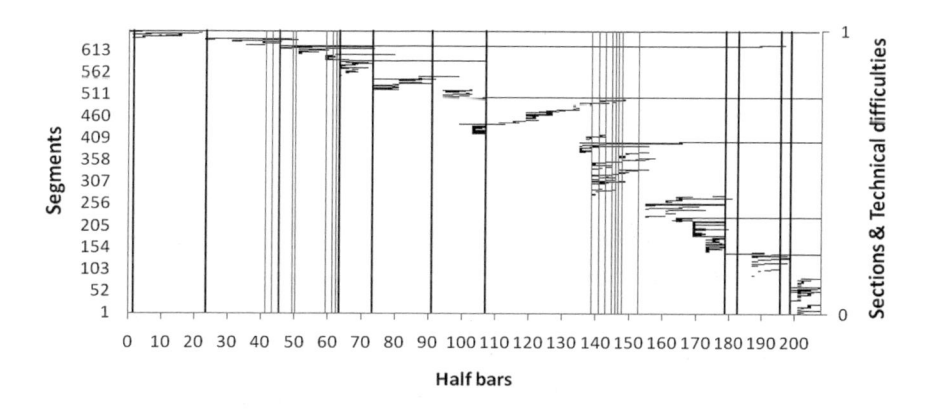

Figure 6. Practice graphs for session 58, showing beginnings of sections (dark lines) and interpretive performance cues (top panel; pale lines), performance cues for fingering (middle panel; pale lines), and technical difficulties (bottom panel; pale lines).

Comments

In preparing for performance, I did not talk much to the camera as it disrupted my concentration. I was focusing on subjective musical intentions and on the projection of musical ideas that were difficult to express. Figure 2 shows that the main change was an increase in the proportion of metacognitive comments. These were mostly negative, dispassionate evaluations of my playing: "Not very clean"; "Sounds flat"; "It's no good"; "I'm concentrating on the bits that I heard on the last recording (of the recent concert) which were not good at all in terms of intonation." Cleaning up problems of this sort was an important part of preparing for performance.

CONNECTING THEORY AND PRACTICE

Seeing the 'big picture'

The noted pianist and pedagogue Heinrich Neuhaus suggests that when a great musician first approaches a new piece, "an instantaneous and subconscious process of 'work at the artistic image' takes place" (Neuhaus 1958/1973, 17). Neuhaus's dictum points to an important characteristic of expert problem-solving: experts start with the big picture. For example, when a mathematician or physicist tackles a new problem, she or he starts by identifying underlying principles. If these are not immediately evident, time is taken to develop a deeper understanding of the issues before proceeding. The steps then taken towards solving the problem are guided by this big picture. Novices, in contrast, plunge into the details without developing a clear idea of the big picture. As a result, their understanding of problems is more superficial and their efforts in problem-solving less effective (Glaser and Chi 1988; Chi, Feltovich and Glaser 1981).

In similar fashion, Neuhaus suggests that a musician's first goal in approaching a new piece should be to develop an "artistic image" of its musical shape (Neuhaus 1973, 7–29). The artistic image guides detailed decisions with regard to technique and interpretation (Chaffin et al. 2003). Our study of the Prelude shows how the process works when the music is difficult to play fluently at the outset. Of course, I was familiar with this Prelude, one of the best-known works of the cello repertoire, but I did not have strong preconceptions about how to play it. I wanted my "artistic image" to develop with my cello and bow in hand. We have seen how my decisions about technical and musical issues were interwoven throughout my learning of the Prelude.

At the end of the study I was gratified to discover that I seemed to have followed Neuhaus's advice. From the outset, my practice was organised around the musical structure. In other words, I was thinking about the general musical shape of the piece (Chaffin et al. 2003). I also gave priority to developing my artistic image for the piece over solving its technical difficulties. Intensive practice during the initial exploratory stage was directed at developing my interpretation and building the dynamic contrasts implied by the score. I did not invest in intensive practice of the technical difficulties until I was sure that my musical ideas were going to work—not until the stage of preparing for performance.

At the time, however, musical and technical issues were scarcely separated in my mind. It was not until I saw the analyses of the early practice sessions that I became aware that my playing was directed much more by my emerging musical image than by technical issues. In retrospect, I can now see how tensions between the two are reflected in the divergence between what I did and what I said.

Words vs. actions: two windows on the mind

Although my commentary focused very little on my musical image of the piece, the plan announced in session 3 did recognise its importance: "I have to decide musically what I want and then I can choose a fingering." Why did I not mention this plan again? Perhaps, in answer, I might ask you, the reader, why you are reading this chapter: what is your plan? Perhaps you are interested in processes of music cognition, or hope to improve your practice technique. Whatever your answer, though, you may not have explicitly formulated your intentions until just now. The goals that direct routine activities are normally implicit (Wegner and Vallacher 1986, 559–563).

I was capable of articulating my goals—this one, at least—but mostly they remained implicit. The feeling slowly evolved that my musical intentions could successfully be articulated technically. This started to take hold during the listening stage and solidified in the re-working stage. Meanwhile, my comments focused on technical problems, both because they were easier to put into words and because I knew that, ultimately, technical matters would influence the musical outcome. Practice and commentary provide different windows into a musician's mind; both are important.

Reflection-in-action vs. reflection-on-action

Inevitable tensions arose between my roles as artist and research participant, and these needed constant management. Deep reflection upon the artistic processes can disrupt the flow of artistic work, a risk of reflection-in-action (Schön 1987). It is possible to overdo conceptual preparation and I had to be careful not to let this happen. Sometimes I mentally withdrew from the project in order to re-establish my musical relationship with the piece. In addition, the research required certain activities that do not form a normal part of everyday practice: talking to the camera, articulating ideas explicitly, and reacting to questions from the team of researchers. At times, these activities made the whole process feel slightly artificial.

Providing reports of my musical decisions and understanding—reflection-on-action (Schön 1987)—was extremely difficult. I had to exteriorise feelings and intuitions about the music that normally remain tacit. While valuable in the long run, this was difficult to do at the time. Sometimes, talking to the camera (and changing tapes) interrupted the flow of musical ideas; this may explain why the number of comments diminished considerably as the first performance approached.

On the other hand, the strains imposed by the nature of the project have had beneficial effects. Firstly, the objective picture I gained of my practice has increased the efficiency and focus of my practising of other repertoire. Secondly, understanding how I memorise music has made the process faster, more solid, and more confident, leading me to rely more on a conceptual approach. Thirdly, at the time, the effort of noting musical decisions on the score helped to consolidate my musical ideas. Finally, knowing how starts and stops during practice affected the PCs necessary for memorised performance led me to vary my practice, starting and stopping at less predictable places.

Tânia Lisboa, Roger Chaffin, Topher Logan

CODA

I hope that this description of my practice will encourage others to undertake similar studies. Systematic self-study is a good route to improving the effectiveness of one's practice. Self-reflection deepened my understanding of my musical goals for the Prelude, and subsequently my practice has become more efficient. However, these methods are not for the fainthearted; they are demanding. The outcome of this project was, nonetheless, a happy one. The mysteries of performance were transformed, not destroyed, by the scrutiny of the scientific method. For those prepared to put in the time and effort, I believe that practice-based artistic research of the sort described here provides a path to both personal improvement and more effective pedagogy.

REFERENCES

Chaffin, Roger, and Gabriela Imreh. 2001. "A comparison of practice and self-report as sources of information about the goals of expert practice." *Psychology of Music* 29: 39–69.

Chaffin, Roger, Gabriela Imreh, and Mary E. Crawford. 2002. *Practicing Perfection: Memory and Piano Performance*. Mahwah, NJ: Lawrence Erlbaum Associates.

Chaffin, Roger, Gabriela Imreh, Anthony F. Lemieux, and Colleen Chen. 2003. "'Seeing the big picture': Piano practice as expert problem solving." *Music Perception* 20: 461–485.

Chaffin, Roger, and Anthony F. Lemieux. 2004. "General perspectives on achieving musical excellence." In *Musical Excellence: Strategies and Techniques to Enhance Performance*, edited by Aaron Williamon, 19–39. Oxford: Oxford University Press.

Chaffin, Roger, Tânia Lisboa, Topher Logan, and Kristen T. Begosh. 2010. "Preparing for memorized cello performance: The role of performance cues." *Psychology of Music* 38: 3–30.

Chi, Michelene T. H., Paul J. Feltovich, and Robert Glaser. 1981 "Categorization and representation of physics problems by experts and novices." *Cognitive Science* 5: 121–125.

Czerny, Carl. 1970. *On the Proper Performance of All Beethoven's Works for the Piano*, edited by Paul Badura-Skoda. Wien: Universal Edition A.G.

Demos, Alexander, and Roger Chaffin. 2009. "A software tool for studying music practice: SYMP (Study Your Music Practice)." Poster presented at the European Society for the Cognitive Science of Music (ESCOM), Jyväskylä, Finland.

Ericsson, K. Anders, Ralf T. Krampe, and Clemens Tesch-Römer. 1993. "The Role of Deliberate Practice in the Acquisition of Expert Performance." *Psychological Review* 100 (3): 363–406.

Ericsson, K. Anders. 1997. "Deliberate practice and the acquisition of expert performance: an overview." In *Does Practice Make Perfect? Current Theory and Research on Instrumental Music Practice*, edited by Harald Jørgensen and Andreas C. Lehmann, 9–51. Oslo: Norges musikkhøgskole.

Ericsson, K. Anders, and Herbert A. Simon. 1980. "Verbal Reports as Data." *Psychological Review* 87: 215-249.

Ginsborg, Jane, Roger Chaffin, and George Nicholson. 2006. "Shared performance cues in singing and conducting: A content analysis of talk during practice." *Psychology of Music* 34: 167–194.

Glaser, Robert, and Michelene T. H. Chi. 1988. "Overview." In *The nature of expertise*, edited by Michelene T. H. Chi, M. J. Farr, and Rober Glaser, xv-xxviii. Hillsdale, NJ: Erlbaum.

Gruson, Linda M. 1988. "Rehearsal Skill and Musical Competence: Does practice make perfect?" In *Generative Processes in Music: The Psychology of Performance, Improvisation and Composition*, ed. John A. Sloboda, 91–112. Oxford: Clarendon Press.

Hallam, Susan. 1995a. "Professional musicians' approaches to the learning and interpretation of music." *Psychology of Music* 23: 111–128.

Hallam, Susan. 1995b. "Professional musicians' orientation to practice: Implications for teaching." *British Journal of Music Education* 12: 3–19.

Hallam, Susan. 1997. "What do we know about practising? Towards a model synthesising the research literature." In *Does Practice Make Perfect? Current Theory and Research on Instrumental Music Practice*, edited by Harald Jørgensen and Andreas C. Lehmann, 179–231. Oslo: Norges musikkhøgskole.

Lisboa, Tânia, Roger Chaffin, Adrienne G. Schiaroli, and Abby Barrera. 2004. "Investigating practice and performance on the cello." In *Proceedings of the 8th International Conference on Music Perception and Cognition*, edited by Scott D. Lipscomb, Richard Ashley, Robert O. Gjerdingen, and Peter Webster, 161–164. Evanston IL: Northwestern University.

Lisboa, Tânia. 2008. "Action and thought in cello playing: An investigation of children's practice and performance." *International Journal of Music Education* 26: 243–267.

Miklaszewski, Kacper. 1989. "A case study of a pianist preparing a musical performance." *Psychology of Music* 17: 95–109.

Neuhaus, Heinrich. 1973. *The Art of Piano Playing*, translated by K. A. Leibovitch. London: Kahn & Averill. (Original work published 1958).

Nielsen, Siw G. 1999. "Learning strategies in instrumental music practice." *British Journal of Music Education* 16 (3): 275–291.

Nielsen, Siw G. 2001. "Self-regulating learning strategies in instrumental music practice." *Music Education Research* 3: 155–167.

Rubin-Rabson, Grace. 1941. "Studies in the psychology of memorizing piano music: VII. A comparison of three degrees of overlearning." *Journal of Educational Psychology* 32: 688–696.

Schön, Donald A. 1987. *Educating the Reflective Practitioner.* San Francisco, CA: Jossey-Bass.

Wegner, Daniel M., and Robin R. Vallacher. 1986. "Action identification." In *Handbook of Motivation and Cognition: Foundations of Social Behaviour*, vol. 1, edited by Richard M. Sorrentino and E. Tory Higgins, 550–582. New York: Guilford.

Williamon Aaron, Elizabeth Valentine, and John Valentine. 2002. "Shifting the focus of attention between levels of musical structure." *European Journal of Cognitive Psychology* 14: 493–520.

ACKNOWLEDGEMENTS

We thank Alexander Demos for help with the practice graphs, which were produced by SYMP (Demos and Chaffin, 2009).

II.
Performer's harmony: towards a performance of Elliott Carter's Piano Sonata

ALESSANDRO CERVINO

PRELIMINARY REMARKS

One of the most frequently used terms within this article is the verbal formulation 'to practise.' I employ it with the meaning familiar to performers of Western art music: to do, or imagine doing, a set of interrelated activities on a musical instrument (or with the voice in the case of singers) in order to learn to play (or sing) a composition. Each time I use this verb, I am referring to directed effort that has the intended effect of substantially improving the practitioner's performing. As is easy to imagine, such efficient practice is not possible without some kind of reflection. Do not instrumental teachers often warn their pupils against mechanically practising a given passage? Are not the majority of pianists aware of the necessity of concentrated and well-organised practice for making progress? Therefore, in this article the verb 'to practise,' employed in the sense specified above, implies an exercising of the musicians' will to improve qualitatively their level of performance, and refers to a set of activities led by some kind of reflection.

GETTING STARTED

This article focuses on my experience of practising Elliott Carter's Piano Sonata (1945-6, revised 1982). However, it is not an exhaustive account of my learning process. Although descriptions of performers' study experiences can be interesting, they generally require more space than this piece permits. Hence, I prefer to focus on one specific issue likely to stimulate further discussion.

I concentrate on one of the problems encountered at an early stage of practising Carter's Sonata—one that temporarily inhibited my making further performance choices. My difficulty was not that I did not know which to choose from among a given set of performance possibilities, but that these possibilities themselves were potentially infinite. What I needed first was not a set of criteria for making decisions, but rather some points of reference for limiting or, more correctly, for better defining the performance options at my disposal.

In order to avoid any misunderstanding, I should clarify what I mean by 'infinite' possibilities. To those who believe that a performer has to respect a composer's indications faithfully (and I am one of those), the claim that there is an infinite number of possible realizations of a score might seem somewhat heretical. However, in this article I employ the word 'infinite' in the mathematical sense, as in the axiom "between one and two there are *infinite* numbers." Musical signs convey performance instructions which should, of course, be followed. Nevertheless, much of the time these instructions function within a score as illustrations of what should *not* be done. For example, the only prescription the dynamic indication *f* provides beyond controversy is not to play as softly or as loudly as possible (since *f* is not *ff*). Beyond this, every performer knows that the ways of playing *forte* are infinite. The dynamic *f* is contingent upon the musical context in which it is found, the style of the composition, the kind of instrument for which it was written, and so on. Even though the range of possible realizations can sometimes seem quite narrow, infinite variation is still possible within this range. Therefore, to affirm that a score can be realized in infinite ways is not to claim that 'anything goes.' It is rather a consequence of the fact that "even if all the composer's determinative indications are followed to the letter, many matters that must be settled in generating a performance are not covered by them, being left to the performer" (Davies 2001, 209).

To resume the thread of my story: at an early stage of practising Carter's Piano Sonata, I encountered a problem which could not easily be resolved. In response, I chose to do what many performers do in similar circumstances: to start practising and see what happens. As my learning process developed, I gradually realized that not only was I finding a solution to my performance issue, but I was also changing my understanding of certain aspects of the Sonata. More precisely, I was articulating certain features of the composition in a manner quite different from the approaches instilled by my theoretical conservatoire training.

In the forthcoming pages I detail this process, drawing conclusions and showing how the knowledge acquired through the practice of practising moves beyond the simple acquisition of performance skills.

Alessandro Cervino

THE PROCESS

At the beginning of my learning process, the issue at the heart of this article could have been expressed through a very simple question: in Carter's Piano Sonata, when does one chord end and the next begin? Before proceeding, it is necessary to define precisely in which sense the word 'chord' is employed in this text. Generally, the word 'chord' indicates "a combination of two 'according' or harmonious notes sounded *together*" (OED; emphasis mine). However, I use this word as intended by Carter. In an interview with Jonathan Bernard, it is clear that Carter considers the word 'chord' to include "the linear presentation of notes" in addition to any more obvious harmonic implications arising from vertical alignment (Bernard and Carter 1990, 203). In what follows, I will further extend this linear notion of 'chord' in terms related to the experience of a performer.

In order to explore the question "when does one chord end and the next begin?" it is interesting to consider bars 144-145 (example 1). In this passage the tones are chordally ambiguous; they could be understood to form different chord combinations. On the excerpt of the score reproduced in example 1, I have marked triangles, squares and circles respectively below the first of various sequences of notes that might each be considered to form a discrete linear chord. Each row of similar signs corresponds, therefore, to a possible approach to note grouping. This is not exhaustive; other options would be worth taking into account, were the aim to produce a full map of the harmonic potential. However, for my purposes, limiting the analysis to these three combinations is sufficient and clearer than a more exhaustive approach.

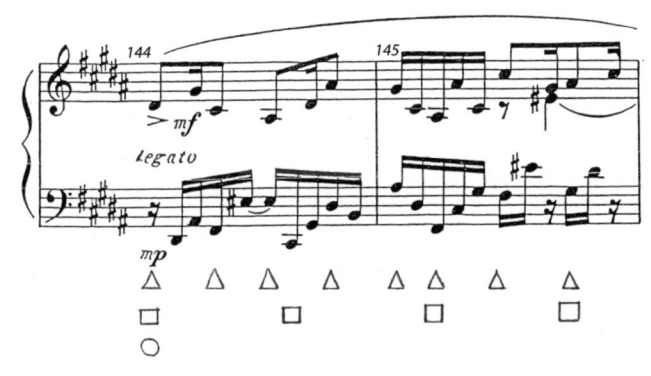

Example 1. Elliott Carter, Piano Sonata, first movement, bars 144-145.
© 1948, 1982 Mercury Music Inc. Used by permission of Theodore Presser Company.

THE PRACTICE OF PRACTISING

Choosing one chordal grouping rather than another from among these three options inevitably leads me to adapt the pedalling, the attack, and the articulation and, consequently, leads to a particular resultant sound. The effect on the pedalling is evident. Since the sustaining pedal of the piano prolongs each tone, it is common practice to change it on the first of any succession of notes that is considered to imply a new chord. Consequently, each row of circles, squares and triangles can equally be understood as a pedal indication. Similarly, the attack—the manner of depressing the keys—varies according to the chosen reading. For instance, following the triangles results in holding the notes at the pedal changes very slightly longer; otherwise, their resonance is not caught by the pedal at this fast tempo and, subsequently, the notes do not sound as part of the harmony.[1] Finally, in this realization the most appropriate articulation is inevitably an overall *legato*, or else all tones would sound separated, even with the pedal.

These different interpretations of the harmonic plan therefore influence a range of performance parameters. The question then becomes how to choose between different possible realizations.

From the above, it would seem that once an approach to grouping notes into chords has been decided upon, the performance problem is resolved. If this were the only issue encountered in relation to the harmony, deciding how to play the piece would become quite an easy business. However, the more I practised this sonata, the more I realized that understanding when one chord ends and the next begins was actually just the most superficial aspect of a more complex matter. The process through which I acquired this awareness started from the moment I turned my attention to how I was balancing the different voices. For instance, in bars 14 to 17 (example 2), I noticed that I tended to give a prominent role to the bass, considering the most recurrent notes of each bar, or of each beat, as a chord and trying to focus my listening towards them. This approach shared commonalities with my practising of earlier compositions from the piano repertory.

I asked myself whether this was the only possible manner of balancing the tones of the passage. As might be expected, by trying alternatives I discovered many possible solutions. For example, when I changed the pedal at the beginning of bar 17, the first chord sounded 'empty.' However, it was also possible to merge

---

[1] This is not a matter of tempo but of how long the key is held down. If the note is released too quickly, the damper silences the note before the pedal can work.

Alessandro Cervino

the end of bar 16 elegantly into the beginning of bar 17 by not releasing the pedal completely.[2]

Example 2. Elliott Carter, Piano Sonata, first movement, bars 14-17.
© 1948, 1982 Mercury Music Inc. Used by permission of Theodore Presser Company.

This and many other similar passages in the movement made me question my traditional way of considering harmony. I gradually came to a different and, at least for me, more fruitful way of thinking, perceiving harmony as a sound field in continuous transformation rather than as a succession of chords, each with sharply defined boundaries. Of course, in any one passage some notes are more prominent than others, but every note influences the harmonic course of a musical work. This is especially true in the context of Carter's free-flowing piano writing, with its continuously evolving and transforming sound combinations. Considered this way, the harmony is constantly being shaped by the performer, when playing, in relation to the possibilities offered by the score. From this perspective, simply

---

2   The sustaining pedal is not a simple binary switch. In a good concert piano, its movement corresponds to an opposite movement of the dampers. Therefore, the smaller the depression of the pedal, the less the dampers rise and the shorter the duration of the strings' resonance. When the pedal is not completely released during a pedal change, the tones resonate sufficiently to enrich but not fully to interfere with the harmonic resonance of those that follow.

THE PRACTICE OF PRACTISING

to know when a chord begins and ends is not especially helpful. Instead, the main issue becomes: how can the harmony of this composition best be described from a performer's point of view; how is it determined by performance? Or better: can something be said about the harmony which can function as a point of reference within the finite field of infinite performance choices?

In the forthcoming paragraphs, I employ the phrase 'chord field.' As above, 'chord' is meant in Carter's sense (1990, 203), as a group of interrelated notes played simultaneously and/or presented in succession.[3] I add the world 'field' in order to reduce the sense of clear harmonic definition that the word 'chord' alone may suggest. For example, the sentence "in this bar there are two chords" makes sense and does not need further explanation. However, the proposition "in this bar the first chord evolves and gradually becomes the second" implies something more complex. Indeed, if a chord is evolving, then some of its sounds change. From the moment its sounds change, in a harmonic language in which ambiguities do not allow us to consider certain notes as secondary, the chord becomes a different one. Therefore, what is the sense of saying that "a chord evolves and gradually becomes another chord"? By adding the word 'field,' I intend to avoid this paradox. A chord field has its specific underlying colour. This is shaped by foregrounding certain notes when playing. At the same time, all other notes can be articulated so as to enrich and/or gradually and continuously transform the chord field's specific colour. At a given point of its evolution, a chord field can no longer be considered to retain its original identity, and a different group of notes starts to be identified as characteristic of a new chord field. We might compare this to a field of grass in which one plants a tree. The field remains recognized as such despite the tree. However, after planting a certain number of trees, the field would more likely be defined as a wood. This forestation can be immediate, by planting hundreds of developed trees; or it can take many years if the trees grow from seedlings and nature is allowed to take its course. Similarly, a chord field can be identifiable for a short period (even if mixed with other sounds) and can gradually fade into the next field or immediately be interrupted by it.

Armed with this definition, I shall now explain how I answered the new questions. During practice, I noticed that when I had to make decisions that

---

3   Theorists of twentieth-century music generally prefer in such cases to use the more generic word 'set' in order to avoid confusion with the more general understanding of a 'chord' as a group of notes played simultaneously. However, Carter dismisses this distinction: "'set' is a word for tennis not for music" (Bernard and Carter 1990: 203).

would influence the subtleties of the harmonic resonance, I focused on the chord fields and particularly on the ways in which they could change form, the velocity with which this could happen, and what I call the loose or blended character of the fields.

To illustrate the first feature, I shall take as an example bar 84 (example 3). This bar includes all twelve tones with the exception of F and B-flat. The musical context makes it possible to play this bar with pedal, and to stress the harmonic rather than the contrapuntal qualities. As can be inferred from the above, individuating the chord fields has an effect on the pedalling. However, the reverse is also true. While practising, I noticed that holding the pedal for the whole measure did not give a satisfying result (at least to my ears); all sounds were excessively blurred. Therefore, it was better to distinguish at least two chord fields in this bar, the second beginning from the triangle (the B; see example 3, below).

This choice was initially arbitrary; it was a consequence of trying out this passage on the piano. Yet by looking at the score, I could formulate a hypothesis to support the decision. The first four notes of the melody in the middle of the texture (starting from the E-flat) are all flattened, in a context where the four flats of the key signature have otherwise been changed to naturals; the next four are all naturals, conforming more closely to the notes that accompany them. This implied a chromatic shifting between notes four and five of the melody, which gave a confused result if the first four notes were allowed to resonate through the final minim of the bar. One might object that it is better to change the pedal one note after the triangle, to avoid the F-sharp and B of the upper voices interfering with the tones that follow. I would counter this by arguing that to change the pedal at that point impoverishes the harmonic texture. However, with further practice

Example 3. Elliott Carter, Piano Sonata, first movement, bar 84.
© 1948, 1982 Mercury Music Inc. Used by permission of Theodore Presser Company.

I found that my idea—to distinctly change the pedal on the B—was not the best solution. Indeed, such pedalling cut off the previous tones roughly and disturbed the character of this passage. I found that I preferred to merge the boundaries of the chord fields slightly by a use of the pedal similar to that for bars 16–17 (see example 2) and by means of a particular approach to touch—for example, by employing the more fleshy part of the fingertip so as to obtain a less direct attack of the sound. Since, as a performer, I often have to choose whether to stress the boundaries of a chord field clearly or to merge them, this distinction can function as a point of reference for making performance choices relative to other parameters: for example, for determining the most appropriate pedalling action, approach to touch, and so on.

The second aspect of the harmony which it is fruitful to describe is the velocity with which chord fields follow one another. In many passages of this sonata, performance choices have a decisive influence on this parameter. As explained above, bars 144–145 (example 4) could be played in several ways. For example, they could be considered as one chord field. However, it is also possible to vary the harmonic texture far more and to draw out certain subtler changes. In this case, the chord fields are short and follow one another much more closely; the boundaries of this second version are represented in example 4 by means of broken lines. The two versions imply two different pedalling actions and approaches to touch. Indeed, as before, if I change the pedal quickly, I have to hold the first notes of each field slightly longer and stress them a little bit more, in order not to lose their resonance.

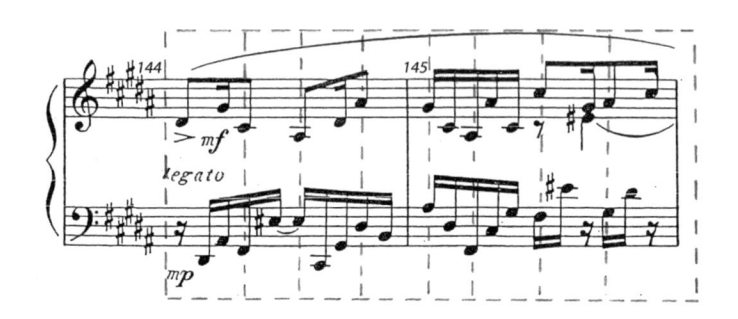

Example 4. Elliott Carter, Piano Sonata, first movement, bars 144-145.
© 1948, 1982 Mercury Music Inc. Used by permission of Theodore Presser Company.

Alessandro Cervino

The final point of reference for making performance choices is perhaps the most obvious. Until now, I have explored how sequences of notes can be considered as chord fields. However, to emphasize the harmonic value of a musical passage is not always interesting or appropriate. Sometimes it is more fitting to stress its melodic characteristics, drawing out the counterpoint of lines. As I will explain below, the choice between melody and harmony depends on the shape one intends to give to the unfolding of the music. In Carter's Piano Sonata, many passages allow for alternative interpretations. For instance, in bars 134–137 (example 5), if I wanted to highlight the interweaving of lines I would play with very clear articulation and almost without pedal. Conversely, if I wanted to make the harmonic texture audible, I would employ a softer attack, keep my fingers more closely in contact with the keyboard, keep my wrists and hands very relaxed, and make much greater use of the pedal. I describe this latter harmonic result as *blended*, and the former approach as *loose*.

Example 5. Elliott Carter, Piano Sonata, first movement, bars 134-137.
© 1948, 1982 Mercury Music Inc. Used by permission of Theodore Presser Company.

These three approaches to the harmonic aspects of Carter's *Piano Sonata* are not intended as fixed categorizations. Indeed, it would be disingenuous to state, for example, that a performer can play with an approach that is either completely blended or completely loose. Instead, I am proposing these opposites as points

THE PRACTICE OF PRACTISING

of reference. One's playing of a given passage can tend towards the extreme position of either category, depending on the interplay between the musical context, the interpretation of the composer's instructions, and the performer's taste preferences. To define my approach to playing a given passage as blended is not, for example, to suggest that I would play all blended passages in an identical way. The same can be said of all other categories.

In terms of my three approaches to articulating harmonic characteristics, many passages in the Carter Piano Sonata can quite appropriately be played in different ways. However, there are sections where the score does not allow such freedom. The first four bars of the second movement (example 6) are an example of this. The relatively slow tempo and the homophonic writing make it impossible to play this passage with a fast-changing harmony and a loose texture. It would be possible to blur the boundaries of the chord fields, but this would be decidedly awkward in its contradiction of the chorale-like writing of these bars.

Example 6. Elliott Carter, Piano Sonata, second movement, bars 1-4.
© 1948, 1982 Mercury Music Inc. Used by permission of Theodore Presser Company.

Despite examples such as this, the majority of passages in this composition can be played in several ways, even while fully respecting the instructions given in the score; I have examined some of this through examples 2–5. Acknowledging this potential variety can constitute a starting point for making large-scale performance choices. Indeed, in addition to reflecting how one prefers to shape the unfolding of the musical ideas at any given moment, the manner of playing passages where the score admits of a variety of possibilities can be decided according to their relationship to those passages without such ambiguities. For instance, bars 36–38 (example 7) should be played loosely: the transparency of their polyphony is too evident to be overshadowed by the harmonic texture it can generate. The melody is an important element of the first movement and appears here for the first time. It is therefore justifiable for a performer to wish to make this passage sound as a surprise or as a striking focal point. He or she might achieve this by, for example, playing the first thirty-five measures in a blended way and with slowly changing chord fields. After this passage, the performer might move from a loose harmonic texture to a blended one, shifting from fast-changing to slow-changing chord fields with the boundaries increasingly unclear. In this way, within the section from the opening through to bar 83 (where a slower section begins) two different performance strategies will have been used, with bar 36 acting as a turning point between the two.

Example 7. Elliott Carter, Piano Sonata, first movement, bars 35-38.
© 1948, 1982 Mercury Music Inc. Used by permission of Theodore Presser Company.

THE PRACTICE OF PRACTISING: A TOOL FOR KNOWING

In the above, I have verbalized part of my learning process. On approaching Carter's Piano Sonata for the first time, my impression was that its harmony lent itself to multiple readings, and that, to make an interpretation, I needed to form an understanding of the harmony and the distinction between one chord and the next. However, by practising I realized that the issue I was attempting to resolve was not really terribly important for someone whose goal was to perform the composition. Indeed, I noticed that by varying the quality of the attack, the articulation and the pedalling in a coordinated way, I could obtain sound combinations whose subtlety went far beyond that which could be revealed by a theoretical analysis of the harmony alone. From the first stages, then, the practice of practising revealed its power not only to generate an unutterable kind of knowledge—a knowledge embedded in the performance—but also to influence ideas about the composition which *could* then be expressed verbally.

The first conclusion formulated was that, for a performer of this work, harmony is a sound field in continuous transformation, rather than a succession of chords. As a performer, I was not primarily interested in this idea for its own sake, but rather for the possibilities it offered for informing and inspiring the practice of practising itself. By following this principle I found three ways of describing the harmony of Carter's Piano Sonata: the first was concerned with whether and how to merge the boundaries of each chord; the second addressed the velocity with which harmony changed; and the final approach helped determine whether to interpret passages harmonically or melodically. Each decision within these categories implies different ways of playing and of listening.

Through a particular practice of practising I have therefore achieved one resolution of the problem set out at the beginning of this article: namely, how to define the performance options at my disposal within a finite range drawn from the virtually infinite possibilities available. In the process, I came to a definition of harmony from a performer's perspective. Articulating my large-scale performance choices according to this definition led to my developing an account of the composition that proceeded from a different basis than that found in the kinds of accounts—primarily musicological—that musicians are used to reading. As a result, the account itself emerged as somewhat different in approach and quality from more traditional readings.

AFTERWORD

The reader may be interested to know which criteria, if any, I employ in order to make performance choices within my system of reference—in other words, why I choose to play a given passage with slowly changing harmony, or to articulate the composition according to any particular strategy. It would be perfectly possible to illustrate my criteria, but I wonder if this is the right context in which to do so. As can be imagined, during my learning process, I have developed my own view of Carter's Sonata—ideas about the composition which reach far beyond the solutions to practical issues described in this article. For example, I have formed opinions about the emotional expressivity of this piece, the character of each musical event, the meanings the piece should convey, the atmosphere that could be created through a performance, and so on. These personal ideas could be expressed through words, forming what Levinson (1993) would call *critical interpretation* and Davies (2003) *descriptive interpretation*. My descriptive interpretation of Carter's Sonata informs my performance. However, to express it in the context of this article would be problematic.

I have attempted to give an honest and rigorous account of my artistic practice: "honest" since I have described what really happened during my learning process; "rigorous" since, even though the content of this article derives from my personal experience, what I write could be verified at the keyboard by anybody who plays the piano proficiently. To expound my descriptive interpretation of Carter's Sonata and to claim it as the basis of my performance choices would be equally honest, since it represents what I truly believe. However, it would not be rigorous, since my assertions could not be verified. As Levinson and Davies argue, there is no one-to-one relation between any verbalized interpretation of a musical work and the way in which it is played; Levinson and Davies call the latter *performative interpretation*. Indeed, "different performative interpretations might be equally consistent with and illustrative of a given descriptive interpretation of the work, and different descriptive interpretations might be compatible with and exemplify a single performative interpretation" (Davies 2003, 255). Since these two kinds of interpretation of a composition "are logically distinct sorts of things" (Levinson 1993, 36), any apparent relation that I might show between my verbally expressible ideas about Carter's Sonata and my performance choices would, strictly speaking, be arbitrary.

This does not mean my verbally expressible ideas on the composition are bound to remain mute and 'secret.' There are other contexts in which their articulation would not only be suitable but might even be desirable: a piano lesson, for example. This particular context for knowledge dissemination has conventions different from those of a publication. In a piano lesson, there is generally only one receiver at a time: the student. Furthermore, the information to be conveyed is selected according to the following, largely utilitarian, criterion: good advice is that which helps the student play better. In this context, to speak about any idea, musical or not, which can inspire or inform a performance is legitimate; such ideas feed the student's imagination whether or not they are rigorous and can be verified or contextualized. What matters, instead, is the power of the teacher's utterances to inspire the student and stimulate his or her own personal journey of further discovery through the practice of practising.

As I have illustrated in this article, attending to the practice of practising is a powerful means of acquiring insights into a musical work. However, the results it produces are variable in nature and, consequently, need to be applied differently and appropriately according to context. My research into possible points of reference for performance choices in Carter's Piano Sonata has constituted the subject of this text. By contrast, the descriptive interpretation of the composition which I have acquired by practising would be of more use for pedagogical purposes. Ultimately, though, focusing on the practice of practising has allowed me to learn to play Carter's Piano Sonata. This ultimately personal and ineffable outcome can be disseminated to others only by a public performance of the composition.

REFERENCES

Bernard, Jonathan W. and Elliott Carter. 1990. "An interview with Elliott Carter." *Perspectives of New Music* 28 (2): 180-214.

Carter, Elliott. 1982. Piano Sonata. Rev. ed. (composed 1945-46). Bryn Mawr, PA: Mercury Music Corporation.

Davies, Stephen. 2001. *Musical works and performances, a philosophical exploration*. Oxford: Clarendon Press.

Levinson, Jerrold (1993). "Performative vs. critical interpretation in music." In *The interpretation of music: philosophical essays*, edited by Michael Krausz, 33–60. Oxford: Oxford University Press.

III.
Morton Feldman's Late Piano Music: Experimentalism in Practice

CATHERINE LAWS

In a recent article on the problems of analysing the music of Morton Feldman, Dora Hanninen concludes, "Truly to get at what makes Feldman's music what it is, we must be willing to analyse not only the music but also ourselves—our habits of thinking, hearing, and doing music analysis" (Hanninen 2004, 228). To this I would add our habits of playing, for Morton Feldman's piano music—particularly as represented by his long, late pieces from the 1980s—poses particular challenges to the performer, and the pianist's response to these questions becomes significant to the experience and understanding of the music at every level. The music is rarely virtuosic in standard ways, but in other respects is extremely difficult to perform well. All piano music requires attention to details of touch, tone, dynamics and pedalling, but much of Feldman's music operates within a very narrow, extremely soft dynamic range, often at the borders of what is possible in terms of quiet piano sound, and sometimes over very long periods of time; *Triadic Memories* (1981) lasts around 90 minutes, and *For Bunita Marcus* (1985) little less (although these are by no means Feldman's longest works: *String Quartet II* from 1983 lasts for around five hours).

In *Piano Notes*, Charles Rosen points out that most composers assume a uniformity of tone colour across the piano, when in reality even the most well-balanced piano has very different colours in the lowest and highest regions (Rosen 2004, 45, 50); the fact that these changes are gradual across the range often obscures the significant differences. Feldman's compositional choices in his late piano music reveal a particular sensitivity to this issue, especially in relation to the decay of the sound. He liked to compose at the piano, often with his head very close to the instrument, listening carefully to the decay (Bryars and Tilson Thomas 1996); he said that sound as a physical fact kept him from floating off into an "intellectual daydream," guarding against an abstract compositional idea of how the piece would sound, at some remove from the acoustical reality (Feldman 2000, 206). As a result, the pianist must, perhaps more than ever, scrutinise the quality of the sound she produces, alert to the most subtle relative qualities of sound across considerable lengths of time.

The process of practising and performing Feldman's music throws into stark relief issues that lie at the heart of piano playing, but which often become submerged, elsewhere in the piano repertoire, beneath other concerns. Pianists can often be rather poor listeners (Rosen 2004, 36). Unlike many other musical instruments, the piano is a giant and complex machine that nevertheless requires only a very simple action to produce a relatively pleasing tone. Moreover, when playing denser textures, the involvement of most of the body—especially the upper body—in the act of sound production can make one feel physically involved with the resonance without necessarily paying real attention to its qualities; as Rosen says, "The danger of the piano, and its glory, is that the pianist can feel the music with his whole body without having to listen to it" (Rosen 2004, 19).

Pianists do, of course, focus in their training on details of finger and pedal technique, and on how they influence the quality of sound production. However, the virtuosity of much solo piano music in the Western classical tradition can distract attention from qualities of sound towards the fundamental issue of 'getting around the notes.' With especially difficult music this can become the main aim of practice, and the showmanship of virtuosity can sometimes become the focal point of performance for both artist and audience. This is not to suggest a complete neglect of sound quality, but rather a tendency to be content with a somewhat generalised notion of a 'good' tone (rich and deep, with a singing quality for melodies), subsequently concentrating on other matters rather than on the details of relative sound qualities. The instrument's very versatility, in terms of its melodic, harmonic and rhythmic capabilities, combined with the pre-eminence of the idea of musical form as a logical continuity articulated primarily through these parameters, often leads pianists to concentrate expressive intentions towards form and structure at the expense of sonority, timbre and texture.[1] However, this is not the case with Feldman. I will argue that in playing Feldman's music one is forced to confront the connection between resonance and the perception of form. As such, the pianist's practice when preparing and performing this music is always, self-consciously, part of a process of inquiry that tests the relationship between sounds across time.

---

[1] Pianist Philip Howard, who has recorded Feldman's *Palais de Mari*, puts it more bluntly, stating that in most music, "people have enough to occupy their thoughts and fail to notice the importance of resonance and decay ...., but when it gets sparser they start having to think about it suddenly" (Howard 2010).

Catherine Laws

MEMORY AND SUBJECTIVITY IN FELDMAN'S LATE MUSIC

Feldman's move to composing longer and longer pieces was driven by his sense that musical form had become a "paraphrase of memory" (Feldman 1985, 127); that organic antecedent-consequent structures of any kind resulted in a focus on expectations (and their denial) and on the recognition of returning (while often transformed) materials—that is to say, on processes of memory, rather than on musical sound. In this respect, he argued, there is no difference between the musics of Beethoven, Schoenberg or Boulez (for example); however different the musical language, the qualities of sound are always subsumed into the priorities of construction: "all music for me that is involved with the concept of beginning, middle, and end finally becomes very much the same, because you have to make certain types of moves in this construction" (Feldman 2008, 1:52). By extending his works beyond the usual, assimilable length, he hoped to move listeners beyond any initial expectations that the quiet, uneventful music was bound to grow into something else, and towards a different kind of listening, released from such anticipations and located in a different kind of temporal experience, concentrating attention on the local patterning and resonance of the musical fabric.

This is not, however, a denial of memory, but rather a refocusing on the very ambiguities and uncertainties of memory when it operates outside conventional or received structures. Feldman talked of "formalising a disorientation of memory" (Feldman 1985, 127), and there are two particular, non-musical influences here: Anatolian rug-making and the abstract cross-hatch patterns used by the artist Jasper Johns. Anatolian rugs have repeated patterns, but the rug-makers work on one section of a rug at a time, folding completed sections underneath; the pattern is not referred to directly but is instead held in the memory (unlike in Persian rug-making, where the whole rug is laid out in front of the maker). Thus the patterns tend to be almost symmetrical, but with tiny differences which result from the inaccuracies of memory (Feldman 1985, 124). The technique of abrash—of dying the yarn in small quantities, resulting in slight differences in the depth of colour—adds to this, again causing minor variations across the rugs. A number of writers have made the link between these techniques and Feldman's use of orchestration and chordal clusters,[2] while Feldman himself notes the effect on his rhythmic thinking—the use of "a disproportionate symmetry, in which a symmetrically

---

2 See, for example, Harrison 1996, 16.

staggered series is used: 4:3, 6:5, 8:7, etc., as the point of departure" (Feldman 1985, 124).

Similarly, Jasper Johns' crosshatch works (from 1972 onwards) comprise simple, abstract hatching patterns, wherein no one mark or bundle of marks is more important than any other.[3] The marks are often semi-systematised in some way, structured partly by colour, angle, or changes in material, such that one is drawn into finding patterns across the canvas, but absolute regularity or system is avoided: there is an element of compositional intervention in the system, a blurring of the objectivity of the systematic events with the subjective and apparently intuitive intervention of the artist. Feldman said that his understanding of both Anatolian rugs and Johns' work led him to ask, in musical terms, "When does a pattern become a pattern?" (Feldman 1985, 128); he attributed to Johns his own reconsideration of how repetition or variation might be used (Feldman 2008, 1:450, 1:452, 2:598).[4]

Additionally, early in his career, Feldman was concerned to remove from his work the traces of himself as composer, finding means of making minimal choices so as to let the sounds "be themselves" (in the words of John Cage, at this time a close associate of Feldman (Cage 1966, 10)).[5] He felt that "only by 'unfixing' the elements traditionally used to construct a piece of music could the sounds exist in themselves—not as symbols, or memories which were memories of other music to begin with." (Feldman 1985, 49). One might describe this as an attempt to objectify sounds, to remove them from the composer's (and perhaps also the performer's) subjective inclinations. Gradually, though, Feldman moved away from this position, clearly feeling a need for greater control over his sounds and their patterning in time.[6]

As a result of these attitudes to memory and the composing self, there are aspects of Feldman's music, particularly the later music, which, while never conforming to overarching imposed structures, contain elements of patterning and even some evidence of system in the choice of pitches, harmonies, and their

---

3   Johns used crosshatching in a number of works from 1972 onwards, but Scent (1974) is a particularly good example, employing solely this technique.

4   For more specific discussion of the influence of Jasper Johns on Feldman's music, see Johnson 2002, 217–247, and Laws 2009, 135-158.

5   For a detailed discussion of what might be understood by Feldman's concept of "the sounds themselves" see Hirata 1996, 6–27.

6   In particular, with respect to the concomitant shift in his approach to notation, Feldman said "you can't write *growing* sound with free notation" (Bernas and Jack 2006, 4).

rhythmic distribution. However, these internal relationships are rarely either rigorous or consistent; he adjusts the materials at will, the overriding concern being the effect of one sound after another rather than conformity to a scheme. Feldman spoke of trying to create a sense that there might be remote family likenesses between musical events—reminiscences rather than solid harmonic connections (Feldman 2008, 2:708). The works of the mid-1970s onwards create complex perceptual effects through the use of rhythmic, melodic and harmonic processes that constantly evade pure repetition, presenting fractionally changing materials in ever-different contexts. This both implies and undermines the sense of an ordering consciousness; the music hovers on the borders of being perceptible as ordered. Additionally—and importantly for the context of this essay—performers and/or listeners become intensely aware of their own attempts to find relations in the music, to follow the sound-qualities through time, trying to get a grip on things. In this way, its own perception becomes the subject of the music; it becomes about the very operation and slipperiness of musical memory, and practice becomes, in part, a feeling of one's way around and through this web of unstable associations. The work achieves a peculiar performative quality, as listeners (and performer-listeners) experience the very processes of perception and understanding that are the subject of the work.

THE PROBLEM OF INTERPRETATION

Traditionally in the Western classical context, the notion of the musical act of creation is bound up with composition. In the performance context, we might think of the performer's role as primarily *re-creative* in relation to an idealised concept of a musical work and its physical manifestation in the form of a score. We might then argue about the extent to which that role, in presenting an interpretation of that work, is creative; how the performer's conscious inflections and deviations are creatively meaningful. However, these late pieces of Feldman do not allow us to operate in quite the same way. In order to interpret, we need a relatively stable entity—a notion, however conceptual, of a musical object—to interpret. Here, the dynamic and timbral fragility of Feldman's sound world combines with the uncertainties produced by the almost-patterns on the boundaries of perception to deny the attempt to concretise the idea of the musical work.

Of course, there is plenty of other music that doesn't operate in relation to such a traditional classical model—non-Western musics, popular musics, improvisation, and much recent experimental and avant-garde music in which the relationship between the composer and performer, along with the concept of the 'work,' is very different (and is often subject to scrutiny). However, Feldman's approach is not related to any of these, either. Having experimented in his earlier music with different forms of notation (especially graph notation) and with giving the performer various degrees of autonomy, his mid- and late-period music in many ways returns to a much more traditional, classical framework, with standard notation. Similarly, the musical language of these late works no longer attempts to reject any relationship to earlier classical music—he no longer suggests that we should try to hear individual sounds as free-floating entities "in themselves." Instead, he takes aspects of diatonicism and also traces of atonal, even serial, languages but reproduces them at a distance. For example, there are elements of triadic formulations, but often restructured and certainly without any sense of functionality, and there are times when Feldman is at pains to imply elements of serial thinking,[7] but again without following through—these things have become part of his toolbox, rather than the fundamentals or principles of a musical language.

Structurally, the use of relatively fragmented modules of material, with distant relationships (whether harmonic, metric, rhythmic or textural) but outside of any kind of antecedent-consequent or other discursive structure, and within a relatively uniform, very low dynamic range, both demands and refuses the classical tendency to attempt to understand relationships across time. Beyond even this, Feldman seems to play with the significance of his own agency and authority, tracing the ghost of the compositional self without that consciousness being at all concrete. On the one hand he retains the traditional composer-performer-listener structure, the status of the score, and he reminds us of his presence through some of the more surprising juxtapositions of material. At the same time, the more systemic elements, the fragility of the soundworld, traces of past musics, and, in particular, the structural and material uncertainties, all expose the contingency of musical meaning and implicate performers and listeners as active in constructing their own sense of meaning in each new context.

---

7   This is apparent, for example, in Feldman's opera *Neither*.

Catherine Laws

Overall, what is significant here might be characterised in terms of one of Feldman's own favourite oppositions: neither/nor.[8] The music is neither part of nor fully rejects its own heritage. As such it demands extremely concentrated listening, as one is drawn into the continuity of events but struggles to orientate oneself. The music operates on the boundaries of our expectations and our memories, performing its own ungraspability as a musical object. In this sense, the notion of 'interpretation,' to my mind, becomes problematic. Yet at the same time, the role of the performer is clearly crucial. The pianist is significant as a listening, structuring self—and hence as a creative force. If these pieces invoke, as part of their own meaning, the process of their own perception as sounds in time, the pianist's self-conscious perception and articulation of hearing and sounding that process are also fundamental to this meaning.

PALAIS DE MARI AND THE CONTINGENCIES OF PERFORMANCE

What, then, does this mean for the performer? I will explore this question by concentrating on Feldman's last piano piece: *Palais de Mari*. The title of this piece is taken from a photograph of an ancient ruined palace in East Asia, seen by Feldman in the Louvre Museum. However, the direct impetus for the piece came from Feldman's composition student, Bunita Marcus, who asked him to condense the material and techniques from his longer pieces into a smaller work; although still around twenty-five minutes, *Palais de Mari* is considerably shorter than most of Feldman's other late works.

As in Feldman's other piano music, there is little here in the way of conventional technical difficulty. Similarly to *Triadic Memories* and *For Bunita Marcus*, there are occasional awkward leaps across wide intervals—here mostly for tiny grace notes, always placed well over an octave above the chords that precede and follow; these require conventional practice. Some of the rhythmic changes also require a little attention, so as not to be wrong-footed by the sudden shifts between bar lengths. However, even in this respect the piece is relatively simple, with none of the more complex or irrational rhythmic relationships found elsewhere in Feldman's work. Additionally, on the surface level at least, Feldman's notational practice appears to leave little room for interpretative exploration on the part

---

8 Feldman uses this opposition as the title for one of his essays (Feldman 1985, 79–81).

THE PRACTICE OF PRACTISING

of the pianist. He gives single metronome and dynamic markings that remain unchanged for the duration of the piece, and he indicates the (very few) points at which the sustaining pedal should be raised and lowered to clear the resonance. The specificity of his metrical and rhythmical shifts—sometimes altering the length of an otherwise repeated note, chord or whole bar only fractionally—are such that any durational freedom on the part of the performer will obscure these subtle but important changes (though in practice the differences in performances are nevertheless considerable, as is evidenced by comparison of recordings;[9] the more concentrated and closely defined the soundworld, the more noticeable and significant the tiniest inflections of rhythm or resonance). Instead, the primary focus of technical practice tends to be upon maintaining the soft dynamic across chords of varying shapes and densities, on touch, tone, and the weighting of chords, on the subtleties of key release at this quiet level, and on how to phrase the short melodic fragments.

Example 1. Morton Feldman, Palais de Mari *(1986), bars 1–27.*
© Copyright 1986 by Universal Edition (London) Ltd., London | UE30238. Reproduced by permission.

---

[9] Unlike much of Feldman's work, *Palais de Mari* has been recorded many times. Recordings include those by well-known Feldman performers such as Aki Takahashi, John Tilbury, Markus Hinterhäuser, Stephane Ginsburgh and Marianne Schroeder (who made the first recording), in addition to those by Alan Feinberg, Siegfried Mauser, Ronnie Lynn Patterson, Steffen Schleiermacher, Sabine Liebner, Philip Howard, Andreas Mühlen, and others.

Catherine Laws

The piece comprises small modules of material: sometimes short blocks of one or just a few bars, interrupted by rest bars of different lengths—anything from 3/16 to 2/2. Example 1 shows the opening of the piece. Importantly, the pedal stays down through the 'rests,' focusing attention on the decay of the sound. Other sections comprise extended passages of long chords that are then repeated but transposed slightly (by a semitone, for example) and with the length of each chord in the set extended or shortened by a quaver or a crotchet (as in example 2). Feldman described this piece as a "rondo of everything" (Feldman 2008, 2:594), stating that "everything comes back" and linking his approach to Jasper Johns' idea of repetition: "Do it one way and then do it another" (Feldman 2008, 2:598). Unsurprisingly though, it is only a rondo in the loosest sense; modules, or elements of them, return, but almost always in altered form and without any clear sense of consolidated reiteration. Repetition here always reveals difference, the subtle changes undermining the sense of identity. This produces an impression of the relatedness of events, without any clear implication of causality or unity.

Example 2. Morton Feldman, Palais de Mari *(1986), bars 342–368.*
© *Copyright 1986 by Universal Edition (London) Ltd., London | UE30238. Reproduced by permission.*

Sometimes the relationships between musical events are obvious. Certain chords or modules are echoed by means of techniques of 'almost' repetition—for example with some pitches reordered rhythmically, or with pitch classes displaced across octaves so that the tone and the decay of the sound are somewhat different, or with exactly the same short chordal sequences simply extended or compressed durationally. Less obvious, but perceptible to varying extents, are other kinds of relationships. Feldman makes use of inversions or transpositions of chords or melodic fragments, but often with the rhythmic relationships retained. Similarly, he sometimes uses only very distantly related chords but employs them within repeated gestures of the same, striking quality (for example by alternating them with single grace notes very high on the piano). Finally, metre is itself subject to similar variation, with frequent repetition of the same time signatures (especially 5/8, 3/4 and 2/2) but with the content similar but varied and the bars subdivided in several different ways; Bunita Marcus describes these as "specific rhythmical images that just keep happening" (Feldman 2008, 2:610), indicating that Feldman treats metre as a formal parameter in itself—something that he had recently explored more fully, in *For Bunita Marcus*.

The result is a general sense of relationships between the musical modules, but at subtly shifting levels and with varying degrees of ambiguity, such that they never quite crystallise into anything graspable. Frank Sani reaches a similar conclusion after a thorough analysis of all the possible relationships perceivable from the score; he identifies a complex web of interconnections, some immediately apparent to the ear and others not, but concludes that there is no core group class providing underlying cohesion: "*Palais de Mari* shows a catalogue of playful workmanship, making through-composing into a highly skilled flow of invention, where groups of pitches are inverted, transposed and re-shaped, and where the introduction of new pitches from time to time is instinctively alternated with echoes of previous harmonies" (Sani 2004). On the one hand these modules act almost as images—their focus and brevity makes them discrete and potentially memorable in themselves—but the endless, subtle reconfigurations cause the memory to start to slip. Perhaps a sense of a relation is retained, but exactly what to, and exactly what has changed? As with Johns' crosshatching, or Feldman's Anatolian rugs, the seemingly objective, systemised relationships are undermined by intuitive and unpredictable interventions. Feldman commented, "what I'm doing is exploring what I feel [are] the discrete possibilities of making connections, which sometimes my brain or ears can't make" (Feldman 2008, 2:710).

Catherine Laws

The word "possibilities" seems key here; the relationships are as much potential as real and are manifested as much by the performer and listener's perception of a possible connection as by any definable, material relationship.

In performance terms, the relative uncertainty or stability of these relationships will of course be partly defined by the pianist's performance decisions, developed through practice. To an extent the pianist will explore and come to decisions about touch, tone, weighting of chords, relative stress of notes, exact tempo, and what *ppp* really means; all of this will affect how the performer produces the effect of one sound listening to another internally, across the fabric of the work. On this level, the process of practice is little different from that for any other music, combining technical and embodied factors into developing a sense of how to project the musical continuity; to an extent, the pianist forms an interpretation through the practical experience of working on the music. However, a range of factors militates against the conventional notion of interpretation and, I would argue, leads to a significant shift in the aims and objectives of practice.

I explained above why the notion of interpretation might be problematic in relationship to the difficulty of establishing Feldman's late works as stable conceptual musical objects. With *Palais de Mari*, there is no clear structure or expressive trajectory to represent. In playing the music—in hearing the subtleties of the relationships exposed by the material reality of piano resonance—one quickly comes to realise that the ambiguities of the music and instabilities of the resonances are such that one hears different connections each time; the performer and listener constantly form and re-form associations out of the soundworld, recreating the musical meaning anew, each time, and subjectively. If the music maps a subtly shifting terrain, to attempt to draw a clear line across it by foregrounding certain relationships is to impose a coherence of experience on something that otherwise hovers on the boundaries of tangibility. In this respect, practice cannot, with this music, consist of finding an expressive pathway to be projected in performance. Instead, the repeated playing of the music gradually accumulates awareness of the ways in which the music not only resists concretisation but is in part 'about' its own undecidability, its own contingency and performativity: 'about' the direct experience of sound in the moment of its perception. In this sense, practice allows for a growing understanding and acceptance of the condition of uncertainty and of the ability to attend and react to ever-changing qualities of sound.

Significantly, the pianist's very understanding of the musical relationships is, in part, dictated by factors only discerned in the moment of performance. Pianists always, of course, grapple with the fact that they can never take their instruments with them. Piano performance is always an experimental business. We have to adapt our techniques in relation to the instrument (and the acoustic). We use any available practice time to get to know the piano, but often this time is limited, and only the most well-established and venerated performers—usually of more mainstream classical repertoire—are able to demand the instrument of their choice for a performance, or to work with piano technicians to rebalance the keyboard according to their preferences.

These issues are faced by any pianist playing any repertoire, but the particularities of Feldman's musical material make them especially significant. Aside from the substantial influence of the size and acoustics of the space in which one is performing, the nature of piano sound at very low dynamics varies between instruments, as does the decay. The particular weight and balance of each keyboard is different, and often there is considerable variation across the range; some of this might only be fully realised in the moment of performance. In contrast to the issue of decay, in *Palais de Mari* the more continuous sequences of chords have the effect of building the sound slightly—with the pedal held throughout long passages, some harmonics continue to reverberate despite the soft dynamic level. Even as these die, the resonance can sometimes be reactivated by the relationship to overtones of subsequent chords, but the exact nature of this resonance will vary from one piano to another (especially in relation to how, and how well, the piano is tuned). All of these things will influence how we hear the almost-patterns of Feldman's music, and these elements are not—cannot be—represented in the score: they are appreciable only through playing and/or listening. While in most music these subtleties are peripheral, subtly inflecting the harmonic resonance but without material implications for form, structure, or overall expression, here the fragility of the soundworld and the ambiguities of the musical connectivity are in part derived from the very nature of these resonances.

As a result, as the pianist John Tilbury stresses, the performer is never entirely in charge of the sound: "you play a chord and you can sustain it, by means of the pedal, and then it's really out of your control. You can kill it, by lifting the pedal, but the very complex way that it disintegrates and changes—you have no control over that whatsoever" (Gardner 2006). Moreover, it is these very variations and unpredictabilities in the ways in which the sound aggregates and disperses that,

Catherine Laws

in part, interest Feldman. The performer is still responsible for the sound, but in this context there is no possibility of subjugating the subtle idiosyncrasies of the instrument to the sense of the musical argument or discourse. Here, there can be no distinction between the two. Exactly what constitutes the music here is completely bound up with the material manifestation of the sound, and hence with the performer's touch. The way in which a particular note or combination of notes sounds in the moment of performance must influence the subsequent approaches to other notes. Moreover, the performer's action-perception loop is somewhat altered. In most music, the pianist plays a note or chord, listens to the immediate qualities of that attack (often unconsciously, as part of an embodied process), and prepares for the next, with the actions subtly influenced by the perception of what is heard. However, in *Palais de Mari* (and much of Feldman's other late music), the 'rest' bars, in which the resonances decay, are not merely spaces between sound events (or in which the performer can prepare the next action) but are materially significant in themselves. *How* the resonance decays, and *how* certain overtones fade from prominence and are then reactivated, is of as much interest as the tones activated by the pianist's fingers. Feldman seems to pose the question, what is the musical material: the notes struck by the pianist, or the sympathetic frequencies that rise out of, and fall back into, the bloom of the resonant texture? For the pianist, this question alters the nature of listening and the relationship between action and perception.

The delicacy of the soundworld poses particular difficulties. Pianists practice *pianissimo* technique, but the minutiae of the differences in key and hammer action mean that the technique has to be subtly adjusted for different pianos, and across the range. Again, a few hours of practice on an instrument is insufficient to be absolutely sure of one's touch across the range at this dynamic level. Practising on different instruments can lead one towards deciding on an approach, but not on an absolute level of sound or on exactitude of touch. The performer has to decide how soft is soft: does *ppp* mean absolutely as soft as possible, on the borders of audibility and with the risk that notes may not always sound, or is a degree of projection necessary, allowing for evenness of tone and the clear definition of musical events? This is, of course, a question that pianists (and other musical performers) confront all the time. Often a decision is taken to set the lowest dynamic not at the very quietest one can play, but at the minimum level at which the audience can still clearly distinguish the sounds. However, the alternatives relate more closely to one's attitude towards the situation of performance; a preference for the clarity and uniformity necessary fully to discern the subtle almost-patterns of the musical fabric must be set against the desire not merely to project but truly to perform the fact that this music is, in part, concerned with the very fragility and contingency of instrumental sound. Either way, one reaches a paradox: on the one hand, practice, however important, cannot prepare one for the particular uncertainties of the moment of performing this music and for the need to be alive to the qualities of sound at every instance; but on the other, only through orientating one's practice towards those problems can one truly understand the nature of this issue—the specifics of those contingencies, and the questions of performativity that Feldman exposes.

Certainly, whatever the pianist's decision, the quality of any one chord or short phrase has implications for our sense of the already uncertain nature of its relationship to another; the subtleties of the relationships, because of their fragility, will vary according to the performer's understanding and decisions, but some of these have to be taken in the moment. Kathleen Coessens argues that in any performance the qualities of a musical gesture, physical and sonic, influence in the moment how the next gesture is created (Coessens 2009, 276–7). This is true, but these pieces of Feldman push this to the forefront and make it pre-eminent in the formation of musical meaning—the manifestation of *kairos* (in Coessens' terms) as the taking of the propitious decision in the moment of the particular situation is thrown into relief. I would argue that the need for the pianist to listen attentively and react to sound in the moment is more extreme than in the performance of most other music. Again, practice cannot lead to decisions as to how exactly to play, but rather towards a greater understanding of the resonant variation and consequent relational potential of Feldman's music, and a better ability to play according to what one hears, rather than according to what one expects or plans to hear.

The performer's treatment of metre and rhythm is also immensely significant, again in relation to the perception of pattern, both locally and across time. Despite Feldman's specificity with regard to tempo and duration, in practice, there are inevitable differences between performances, and even the tiniest variations of either tempo or rhythm affect the emphasis—and hence the very subtle similarities and differences that Feldman employs. Again, this is immediately apparent in comparing even the opening few bars of any recordings, in which the impact of the smallest differences in tempi, phrasing and weighting lead to significantly different effects. Within the articulation of metre and rhythm, the performer is caught between two characteristics of this music: its apparent stillness, low rate of incidence and relatively uneventful nature; and its busyness for the performer, both physically, in terms of the often quite fast shifts between registers, and psychologically, due to the need to subdivide even the longest notes in order to be able to manifest their subtle differences. Feldman commented, "When I work I always have the ictus, even on scores that were two-two, three-two, five-four, there is an underlying clock that's going for me to feel the duration of the piece" (Feldman 2008, 1:364). In *Palais de Mari* this is a quaver. Not all pianists keep this inner pulse in the head; this can be inferred from a number of recordings in which the minor differences in durations fail to make themselves felt. More specifically, the Portuguese pianist, Paulo de Assis, comments on working to an inner pulse in the early stages of practising the piece, before abandoning it in favour of counting according to the denominations of the changing metres. For others, however (myself included), the maintaining of this inner pulse is necessary in order to make apparent the subtle shifts in durations; from 7/8 to 2/2 to 9/8, for example.

As Dirk Moelants has shown in a study of Feldman's much earlier and very different *Last Pieces* for piano, performance decisions about the lengths of notes have a significant impact upon the role of memory in the music—on our ability to make connections between sounds (Moelants 2001, 127–8). In this later music, Feldman is often playing with exactly this ability, and the performer's decisions as to the relationship between ictus, rhythm and metre have a profound impact on sound and memory. Again, some of these decisions can be taken in the usual manner, through the practice process, and might be described in conventional interpretative terms. However, the durational decisions are always linked to harmonic reverberation, and are therefore also subject to the contingencies of the moment of performance I have been discussing. Moreover, this relationship produces a peculiar duality for the performer. As explained above, the significance of resonance and decay requires attention and is different on each piano; while the duration between events is determined by Feldman, the precise details of what we hear in that period is not. In this sense, the effect is of time being marked by the decay—slowly and continuously, but at a slightly different rate and with a slightly different quality, in each performance. At the same time, the ictus ticks away, marking time in short, evenly measured periods, oblivious to the uncertainties of the musical content. However, I would argue that this is one of the productive dilemmas produced by Feldman's music: the awareness of measured time set against experiential time, and the impossibility of resolving that duality. The performer has to experience this 'betweenness' without resolving the contradiction; again, this means practising the experience of uncertainty, cultivating an openness to being pulled sometimes more in one direction, sometimes more in the other, and to respond according to the subtleties of the sound in the moment.

Finally, the physical relationship to the instrument becomes an important factor in the performance of Feldman's music, and one that is, again, influenced by practice. In general, there is a tendency to assume that still, quiet music requires physical stillness on the part of the performer. Certainly, Feldman valued this quality in Aki Takahashi's playing: "Takahashi appears to be completely still. Undisturbed, unperturbed, as if in a concentrated prayer. ... The effect of her playing to me is that I feel privileged to be invited to a very religious ritual" (Feldman 2000, 155). At the same time, there are some sections of the music that require fast movements of the hands, sometimes across a considerable distance; the grace notes are a good example. Additionally, some of the chords comprise wide intervals—especially for those with small hands—and control over the balance and tone can be affected by the relative position of the upper body. In this sense, some flexibility of movement is required for optimal control over the sound. Beyond this, though, John Tilbury argues that, in its focusing in on the details of touch and tone, Feldman's music comprises "a radical commitment to the muscular, physical and essentially sensual qualities of the art of performance" (Tilbury 1993). For Tilbury (and I agree), playing Feldman's music exposes the intimate physical relationship to the instrument, eschewing the rhetorical gestures of pianistic showmanship often apparent in performances of other music: "When David Tudor or Cardew played Feldman what you heard and experienced with great intensity was the limb as it performed, the fingerpad—the most erotic part of a pianist's body—and the resulting sound was raw and thrilling. In too many performances one is all too conscious of a culture intervening between body and instrument" (Tilbury 1993).

Even within this, the subtleties of the physical approach to the instrument influence not only the qualities of sound but also the audience's perception of them. As noted above, the 'rest' bars focus attention on the resonance of the chords, and the pianist listens accordingly. However, at some point the pianist also has to prepare the next bar. In music of greater incidence, this is rarely an issue; but here one can change position slowly, through the resonant decay of the 'rests,' or quickly, in the final moment before the next attack. Inevitably, this decision changes things for both performer and audience. Experimenting with this myself, I find that in moving slowly through the duration of the resonance my breathing remains smoother, the preparation of the next notes is unhurried and feels safe, and the overall effect is more still. In contrast, holding the position until the moment before the next attack produces an alternation of stillness (including of the breath) with an intense quickening at the change of note. Additionally, though, this inevitably focuses attention (both mine and the audience's) more on the decay in itself, rather than on the preparation for the next event; without the distraction of physical movement there is nothing to do but to listen to the decay of the sounds: attention is focused on the moment rather than on what follows. Either way, the relationship between listening and movement is deeply embodied, and the aim of practice is to understand this relationship and to decide on the extent to which one wants to, and how one wants to manifest that relationship.

PRACTICE AS AN EXPERIMENTAL PROCESS

Ultimately, while Feldman is generally considered an experimental composer, I am arguing for the practice of practising as an experimental process, defined in Cage's terms (and subsequently elaborated by Michael Nyman) as orientated towards situations with unknown outcomes (Cage 1966, 13; Nyman 1999, 1–30). In this sense, the aim of practice is not to pin things down—deciding how exactly to place a note, weight a chord, or develop a 'reading' or interpretation of a work—but rather to hone the ability to respond to the contingencies of sound in the moment of performance. This is not to dismiss the importance of technique—as should be clear from the above, the ability to respond appropriately is predicated upon a sound technical basis, especially with respect to touch and tone—but rather to recapture the ultimate aim of practice as leading towards an openness to what cannot be planned for, to the undecidability of performance. In this respect, the practice of practising Feldman's music might alter one's ability truly to listen to the sounds of other music and to attend the ways in which these, too, are manifested in the moment of performance.

John Tilbury comments that one of the things that attracted him most to performing Feldman's music was "the idea that every sound had a unique quality and it was pointless and even wrong to try and have some kind of blueprint as to how you were going to perform" (Gardner 2006). He argues that this gives a particular subjective contribution—perhaps a particularly strong sense of creative involvement. Interpretation in the conventional sense has only a minimal role to play, but every performance decision influences the creation of meaning, affecting the ways in which the performer creates—not just reproduces—the "formalising [of] a disorientation of memory." Barbara Monk Feldman argues that, as a result of Feldman's intense attention to the details of instrumental sound, "We come to hear with the composer's hearing in the same way that we come to view an essential part of any great painter's work through the artist's eyes ... we listen with Feldman's ears" (Monk Feldman 1989). To my mind, though, this misses the performative subtleties of his work; it implies that there is only one way to hear (and, by implication, to play) these pieces—as Feldman did—when in fact the filter of Feldman's music offers a perspective on the sheer variety of difference available within apparently the same chord played on the same class of instrument. As Monk Feldman says, listening to Feldman's music "reaches to the core of our own listening experience," reactivating awareness. Practising Feldman's music opens one to Feldman's alertness to the subtleties of piano resonance, and to the spontaneous, uncertain and dangerous conditions of performativity—conditions that many practice regimes are designed to minimise.

The performer is caught in a web of contradictions: between the incidence of sound and its decay, between experiential and measured time, between playing and listening, between music figured as sound objects and its subjective perception. Feldman's music, as Clark Lunberry says, is concerned with "marking and measuring the dimensions of its own vanishing" (Lunberry 2006, 25); it is concerned with sound as always in the process of disappearing. Conversely performance is always marked as presence: live-ness and the creation of sonic incident. To practise with an experimental mindset is to attempt to accommodate these paradoxes, to explore rather than to resolve them, so as to be able to make propitious decisions in the moment of performance. One of Feldman's favourite pianists, David Tudor, commented that he played Feldman "inwards" (Cardew 2006, 59), with a particular, concentrated listening, and that as a result he felt a deep connection to the music. I would argue that this arises from a resistance to stabilising and subsequently interpreting the musical object, in favour of becoming part of the attempt to establish quite what that object *is*.

REFERENCES

Bernas, Richard, and Adrian Jack. 2006. "The brink of silence." In *Morton Feldman Says: Selected Interviews and Lectures 1964–1987*, edited by Chris Villars, 43–44. London: Hyphen Press.

Bryars, Gavin. 1996. "James Hugonin and Music." *Modern Painters* (Spring), 72-73. Excerpted in Gavin Bryans and Michael Tilson Thomas, "Feldman at the Piano." Accessed 12 December 2009. http://www.cnvill.net/mfatpiano.htm.

Cage, John. 1966. *Silence*. Cambridge, MA: MIT Press.

Cardew, Cornelius. 2006, *Cornelius Cardew: A Reader*, edited by Edwin Prévost. Harlow: Copula.

Coessens, Kathleen. 2009. "Musical Performance and 'Kairos': Exploring the Time and Space of Artistic Resonance." *International Review of the Aesthetics and Sociology of Music* 40 (2): 269–281.

De Assis, Paulo. 2009. Interview with the author, 8 July.

Feldman, Morton. 1985. *Essays*, edited by Walter Zimmerman. Kerpen: Beginner Press.

Feldman, Morton. 2000. *Give My Regards to Eighth Street: Collected Writings of Morton Feldman*, edited by B. H. Friedman. Cambridge, MA: Exact Change.

Feldman, Morton. 2008. *Morton Feldman in Middelburg: Words on Music*, 2 vols., edited by Raoul Mörchen. Cologne: Edition MusikTexte.

Gardner, James. 2006. "Interview with John Tilbury." Accessed 15 January 2009. http://www.cnvill.net/mfgardner.htm.

Hanninen, Dora. 2004. "Feldman, analysis, experience." *Twentieth-Century Music* 1 (2): 225–251.

Harrison, Bryn. 1996. "The late works of Morton Feldman." MA thesis, De Montfort University, Leicester.

Hirata, Catherine Costello. 1996. "The sounds of the sounds themselves: analyzing the early music of Morton Feldman." *Perspectives of New Music* 34 (1): 6–27.

Howard, Philip. 2010. Email to the author, 17 March.

Johnson, Steven. 2002. "Jasper Johns and Morton Feldman: what patterns?" In *The New York Schools of Music and Visual Arts*, edited by Steven Johnson. New York and London: Routledge, 217–247.

Laws, Catherine. 2009. "Feldman—Beckett—Johns: Patterning, memory and subjectivity." In *The Modernist Legacy: Essays on New Music*, edited by Björn Heile. Farnham: Ashgate, 137–158.

Lunberry, Clark. 2006. "Departing landscapes: Morton Feldman's *String Quartet II* and *Triadic Memories*." *SubStance* 35 (2): 17–50.

Moelants, Dirk. 2001. "What is slow?: Timing strategies in the performance of Feldman's *Last Pieces*." In *Proceedings of the VII International Symposium on Systematic and Comparative Musicology—III International Conference on Cognitive Musicology*. Jyväskylä: University of Jyväskylä Press, 121–8.

Monk Feldman, Barbara. 1989. Liner notes to Marianne Schroeder, *Morton Feldman: Piano*. Hat Hut 6035.

Nyman, Michael. 1999. *Experimental Music: Cage and Beyond*. Cambridge: Cambridge University Press.

Rosen, Charles. 2004. *Piano Notes: The Hidden World of the Pianist*. London: Penguin.

Sani, Frank. 2004. "Morton Feldman's *Palais de Mari*: a pitch analysis." Accessed 8 September 2009. http://www.cnvill.net/mfsani3/mfsani3.htm.

Tilbury, John. 1993. "On playing Feldman." Originally published as liner notes to John Tilbury, *Morton Feldman: For Bunita Marcus*, LondonHALL docu 4. Accessed 10 February 2009. http://www.cnvill.net/mftilb.htm.

IV.
Alfred Schnittke´s Piano Trio: Learning and Performing

MARIA LETTBERG

INTRODUCTION

The aim of the study

Practice-related investigations in musicology and music psychology have tended to focus on single topics of music making, often drawing on the knowledge of experienced musicians or music students but filtering these through the 'scientific' perspective of the investigator. Despite certain interdisciplinary studies, such as those by Miklaszewski (1989), Hallam (1995), Chaffin and Imreh (2002) and Hultberg (2008), there is still very little research that provides insights directly into musicians' processes of learning and performing. Moreover, the pedagogical literature on musicians' practice is often described as subjective and anecdotal (Reid 2002, 102–103); musicians often seem to be considered magicians, unwilling to reveal their secrets or perhaps simply unable to articulate them (Lehmann, Sloboda, and Woody 2007, 62–65). Parncutt and Troup (2002, 285–286) complain of pianists' complex pseudo-scientific theories of playing and their lack of knowledge of the physics of the piano (Parncutt 2007, 22–24). This criticism is, in my view, fair, but it would be more interesting to understand why some practitioners develop such theories, and why certain "misconceptions" have been so successful and effective for practitioners (Rosen 2002, 26). Of course, the complexity of music-making, and especially the transformation of the musician's imagination into action, poses a serious problem for any researcher; there are many elements that can collectively affect a performance.

The aim of this work is to examine the Piano Trio (for piano, violin and cello) by Alfred Schnittke (1934–1998) through a comprehensive artistic inquiry. My investigation is dedicated to understanding the common experience of musical practice from the musician's point of view—that is to say, from 'inside.' In other words, this is my contribution to research in and through creative practice, as a musician and observer as well as a performer and scholar. I wanted to explore and better understand how a pianist perceives her/his participation in a chamber music group. While recognising the limitations of this kind of investigation and its possible lack of objectivity (Lehmann, Sloboda, and Woody 2007, 11–14), I argue that investigating music in this way can be illuminating, offering a unique perspective on musicianship in its natural environment. My purpose was not to examine preconceptions but to investigate the internal perceptions of a pianist in the chamber music context.

Methodology, duration and research questions

This research applies qualitative methods in order to explain and understand the processes of learning and performing from the pianistic point of view. The study has followed a process of observing and reporting on my own practice, as well as rehearsals of the whole trio and the process of recording the work.

The first part of the data collection includes detailed descriptions of my everyday practice. The physical practice time was approximately 50 hours, but the measurement of 'real' practice time is problematic. It is particularly difficult to measure the time devoted to mental preparation: putting markings on the score, silent reading of the score, imagining playing the music, thinking about the music, reading relevant books, and listening to recordings. All in all, the gestation period, or "incubation period," to use Igumnov's term (Milstein 1961, 79), was approximately 86 days. Besides 11 hours of rehearsal-data collection doubled with video-recordings, there are also 7 hours of recording data doubled with video recordings.

As mentioned above, this investigation began not with a hypothesis but with questions. Who better than musicians themselves can answer questions about what happens behind the "closed doors" (Barry 2000) of practice studios, rehearsal rooms and recording studios? Therefore, I asked myself: "What will happen in the three months between my first acquaintance with Alfred Schnittke's Piano Trio and the final interpretation in the recording studio?". I also had established a number of concrete sub-questions; I did not necessarily expect to find answers to all of these, but they guided my investigation:

1. Do I have any learning strategies?
2. How do I prepare a piece of chamber music?
3. What will happen during rehearsals?

4. How will I develop my interpretation during the rehearsals?
5. How will we achieve a unity of interpretation?
6. Are there differences between preparing for a concert and recording?
7. How will we record this piece?
8. How important is editing in the process of recording?

PREPARATION FOR REHEARSALS AND RECORDING

Background to the Schnittke recording

Before I introduce the main part of the study, I would like to add some details about myself, my musical partners and the Piano Trio. I am a classically trained, professional pianist with extensive experience of playing in ensembles. My colleagues are members of the established Petersen Quartet: the violinist Ulrike Petersen and the cellist Henry Varema. Prior to this project, I had never heard them play; in fact, we had never even met before the rehearsals. When I was invited by Deutschland Radio to record Alfred Schnittke's Piano Trio and Piano Quartet, I was relatively familiar with his musical style. I had recorded the Concerto for Two Pianos and Orchestra, and Music for Piano and Orchestra, but I had not listened to the Piano Trio. Moreover, I began to learn the Piano Trio in parallel with the Piano Quartet, finding the latter much more demanding. The Piano Trio did not pose any technical difficulties, least of all the second movement. However, with time I found myself asking more and more questions about this piece.

As Ivashkin states, "None of his [Schnittke's] works is simply a 'text'; there is also a text within a text, a submerged part of what can actually be seen. It is not just music but also meditation on music, presenting a montage of various types of music" (1996, 123). It is well known that Schnittke preferred to compose for particular musicians who exemplified what he considered a certain style of performing (Ivashkin 1996, 167): Yury Bashmet, Mstislav Rostropovich, Gidon Kremer, Mark Lubotsky, Oleg Kagan, Natalia Gutman, and Tatyana Grindenko, among others. Each has a very strong individual performance presence that combines the highest level of technical accomplishment with a deep emotional expressivity. Furthermore, all these musicians have backgrounds similar to Schnittke's.

The Piano Trio (1992) is an arrangement of the String Trio (1985), which was commissioned to mark the hundredth anniversary of Alban Berg's birth. The String Trio was first performed in the Small Hall of the Moscow Conservatory by Oleh Krysa, Fyodor Druzhinin and Valentin Feigin. The Piano Trio is dedicated to the neurosurgeon A. Potapow, who twice saved Schnittke's life: in 1985, after his first stroke, and in 1991, when Schnittke suffered his second stroke and an urgent operation was needed. Mark Lubotsky, Mstislav Rostropovich and Irina Schnittke were the first musicians to perform the Piano Trio. Gidon Kremer states that this music expresses the quintessence of Schnittke's suffering and his strivings to find a heavenly power that could overcome terrestrial concerns (Ivashkin 1994, 244). Schnittke himself described the String Trio as nostalgically unified (Ivashkin 1994, 78).

By 1971 Schnittke had already written a striking article about "polystylistic tendencies in modern music" (Ivashkin 2002, 87–90). In this article, and in the conversations with Shulgin in 1976 (Shulgin 1993, 99-100), the composer discussed both the technological and psychological preconditions for a polystylistic approach to musical composition; he saw these as comprising an increase in the information content of a work in the form of the "polyphonisation" of art and consciousness. Schnittke distinguished two polystylistic principles: the quotation or adaptation principle—when a composer cites or uses a stylistic element of existing music—and the principle of allusion—a not clearly recognisable but fine associative link to other music. The Piano Trio is a wonderful example of both adaptation and allusion in Schnittke's music. The piece has strong polystylistic aspects: Schnittke includes the rhythm of, and melodic references to, the song "Happy Birthday to You," Znamenny (Orthodox) chant, and music by Berg, Mahler, Schubert, Bach and Shostakovich (using the D–S[E♭]–C–H[B♭] motif often employed by Shostakovich himself). In the second movement of the Piano Trio Schnittke also uses the C major chord as a particular reference point, and the end-without-an-end that is typical of his works; where the music does not have a clear ending point but just 'disappears' meditatively, in a series of repetitions. The Piano Trio is a multifaceted work, a collage of tonal and atonal fragments bound together by elements of traditional sonata form.

Maria Lettberg

Two mapping systems

Miklaszewski (1989), Chaffin and Imreh (2002), Barry and Hallam (2002), and Lehmann, Sloboda, and Woody (2007) all describe the general stages of the process of learning musical works, from the first overview to subsequent progress from smaller sections (or chunks) to larger units. These correspond with my own stages of preparation. However, I think that the process of learning may also usefully be described in terms of Deleuze and Guattari's concept of 'rhizome' (1977, 34–35). The process of learning a piece of music develops in all directions simultaneously—non-hierarchically (rhizomatically), rather than linearly. I see myself as a "versatile learner" (Hallam 1995, 121), using analytic/holistic and intuitive/serialistic strategies of learning interchangeably. According to Krampe and Ericsson (1995, 84–90), my practice is "deliberating practice," strategic and conscious, and according to Wulf and Mornell (2008, 5–7) it is "random practice," in that I switch frequently between different tasks. There is no doubt that, whatever the practice strategies of a professional musician, they must be effective. However, strategies always depend on the time available for preparation, the familiarity of the compositional style and, of course, the musician's preferences. Sometimes we forget that while making music is a very individual process, it is also conditioned by our shared nature, with its inseparable intellectual and intuitive processes of perception.

So: how did I begin work on the Piano Trio? By simply playing it, as would many musicians (Neuhaus 1994, 13–24; Rosen 2002, 54–55). Pianistic intentions are always embodied; we form a deep connection to our instrument, to the physicality of piano playing (Clark 2002, 66–68). The question "what is this music about?" transforms automatically into the answer "how do I actually realise it?" (Miklaszewski 1989, 103). This is, in my opinion, the root of the problem with musicological approaches to scores, which often employ theoretical analyses alone and overlook practical realisation and performative expression. The musical score is a coded, comprehensive idea of the music, combining a mapping of the musical form, an articulation of its language (melodic, harmonic, rhythmic, etc.), expressive cues (phrasing, dynamics, etc.), and an implicit set of triggers for the embodied performance. For me it is axiomatic that a pianist experiences music through the body, but we do not usually think about this, just as we do not think about how our heart works. We begin with the visual orientation, reading and analysing the score, and then immediately transform it into physical, motoric orientation: playing. This then incorporates an aural orientation, as we listen to our playing (Hultberg 2002, 10).

My records shows that, from the beginning, I attempted to gain an overview of the whole piece by playing it through, and that in doing so I tried to grasp the essential meaning of this music—in other words, a conceptual understanding (Wicinski 2003; Lehmann, Sloboda, and Woody 2007, 22–23). The initial encounters with the Piano Trio inspired me and stimulated my practice. With respect to the three instrumental parts—for piano, violin and cello—I made intuitive choices, playing what I considered to be the most important lines. Through repeated playing of the whole piece and certain sections, I developed clearer ideas of the composition, discovered new aspects of, and ideas in, the music, and thereby 'corrected' my previous impressions.

During the process of learning, I made notes on the tempi and the form, identified themes and structures, and made connections to other music from my previous experience. This interpretative process was based exclusively on my practical experience of playing and my theoretical knowledge of music analysis. I worked on details such as fingering, articulation and dynamics, concentrating on the particulars. For me, working on fingering has always been a very important part of the beginning of the learning process. Through fingering I realise my interpretation of the articulation and dynamics (Clarke et al. 1997, 94–101). However, at the same time, fingering, for the most part, is determined by the positions of the hands (Gieseking and Leimer 1972) and the disposition of black and white keys within individual chords and phrases. Recognising and learning the positions of the hands and fingers facilitates visual memorisation (Aiello and Williamon 2002, 167) and can be a great help with complicated, irregular, and in this case often atonal textures. In addition, working with a metronome helped me to correct mistakes and facilitated faster motor learning (Hallam 1995, 123).

Finding the interdependencies of the piano with the violin and cello parts constituted a considerable portion of my practice time. My final goal was "thinking in sound" (McPherson and Gabrielsson 2002, 102–106), imagining the sounds of the violin and cello as I played my own part. It was important for me to read the score away from the instrument and to listen to a recording of Schnittke's String Trio, which is very similar to the Piano Trio. However, in order to avoid direct influence I started listening to other recordings of the Piano Trio only when I considered that my own conception had been formed.

Maria Lettberg

I notated the information concerning the above aspects on the score, using a system of coloured markings comprising both graphics and text. Significantly, I use the same, personal system of marking for chamber music as well as for solo piano repertoire. Aiello and Williamon (2002, 178) suggest using markers of different colours to highlight the various themes or voices and their recurrences in a score. Even Tony Buzan's popular psychological conception of 'Mind Mapping' (Buzan 2001) makes use of both bright colours and visual-spatial markings to make the learning of written material more effective, thus facilitating long-term memorisation and freeing creativity. With these markings on the score, which for me indicate points of specific attention, I create my own mapping of the piece.

Example 1 provides a concrete illustration of my personal system of marking. It is reproduced here in black and white, but I used coloured markings as follows:

    tenuto/staccato—green

    accents—red

    ppp or *pp* or *p*—yellow

    mp—blue

    mf—pink

    f or *f* or *fff*—red

    ○ (white circle)—white keys

    ● (black circle)—black keys

    △ (triangle)—indicates beats in the bar, especially through longer held notes or where the metre changes

The coloured marking system is important in my personal practice processes. However, this first mapping was only useful until the first group rehearsal. At this point, my concentration was fully diverted to aspects of chamber music performance, and previous markings then became disturbing; the new situation required new points of attention. At this stage, I returned to the original black and white score, with minimum indications (and no colours), and created a second mapping focusing on points of chamber performance. Example 2 shows an example from my second mapping system:

Example 1. Alfred Schnittke, Piano Trio, movement 1, page 6.
Alfred Schnittke Trio für Violine, Violoncello und Klavier © Copyright 1992 by Universal Edition A.G., Wien / UE 30163. www.universaledition.com

Example 2. Alfred Schnittke, Piano Trio, movement 1, page 6.
Alfred Schnittke Trio für Violine, Violoncello und Klavier © Copyright 1992 by Universal Edition A.G., Wien | UE 30163. www.universaledition.com

It is important to note that in my solo piano work I usually use just the one, colour-coded mapping; this demonstrates the difference between solo repertoire and chamber music with regard to performance. The complexity—the 'two levels' in the performing of chamber music—is mirrored in the two marking systems. Musicians need the ability "to coordinate the aspects of their own performing (e.g. pitch, rhythm, articulation, loudness) with those of other performers" (Lehmann, Sloboda, and Woody 2007, 177). The first mapping, created during the individual learning process, introduced many aspects of interpretation related to both individual and ensemble playing. The second marking system shows the changes in my perceptions: my full attention was focused at this point on the points of chamber music performance. The fact that I was able to concentrate on these meant that I had indeed already internalised most aspects of my first mapping.

Lehmann, Sloboda, and Woody point out that our "memory creates an internal map of the piece with close attention to the order of the parts" (2007, 76). However, during this process of performing and recording I had in my head a very clear set of points of focus; a kind of mapping of ensemble music-making. These points are, to some extent, indicated in the score, but most are remembered from practising with the trio members. Chaffin and Imreh describe similar thought processes concerning important switching points and expressive cues during performance (2002, 342–348). Not all musicians use markings, but the fact that these stress points are not annotated on the score does not necessarily mean that they do not exist in the mind of the performing musician. Caroline Palmer's experiments, in which musicians were asked to play first and then to mark intentions on the unedited score, show the very strong connection between intentions and mapping musical thoughts (1989, 331–345). In my case, by marking the text, I was externalising my inner musical scheme.

Maria Lettberg

ACHIEVING AFFINITY

Micro and macro levels of learning

In the process of learning Schnittke's Piano Trio I experienced two levels of learning: the *micro* level and the *macro* level. These are partly reminiscent of 'internal' and 'external' focuses of attention (Wulfs and Mornell 2008, 11–15). The micro level comprises the specific details of the playing. The macro level involves a mental attitude to playing in which the focus is on achieving continuity, with expressive details partly automated in the background or present only as temporary points of attention.

This study revealed that the process of individual learning had parallels with that of group learning. Each combined the micro level and the macro level of learning. During rehearsals we worked on both the micro level (short phrases) and the macro level (longer sections) of the music, towards a sense of affinity in our tempi, rhythm, phrasing, articulation, dynamics, and sound qualities. We worked on the music section by section, initially with a metronome, in order to discover, correlate and correct our tempi. In general, this was a kind of "trial-and-error" method of rehearsal (Miklaszewski 1989, 107), with hardly any discussion about how to work. It seemed that our strategies were somehow very similar, but it is important to note that this is not always the case; musicians sometimes have very different opinions about how to rehearse. In my experience there can often be disagreements about tempi, the use of the metronome, and how much to focus on the particular details (among other matters); but, to some extent, both micro and macro levels are always utilised in the process of rehearsal.

According to Friberg and Battel (2002, 210–212) and Lehmann, Sloboda, and Woody (2007, 178), the synchronisation of ensemble timing is an illusion: musicians try to play together but they never truly succeed. Data analyses of performances show that human perception of the simultaneity of musical sounds is highly subjective. However, the idea of using the metronome as an instructive aid to finding an internal pulse, the 'ensemble's clock,' came naturally to all three of us. Furthermore, we played at slower and faster tempi alternately (Milstein 1961, 80–81), experimenting with different variations in timing and, after practising and making decisions, we played through some sections and then immediately evaluated our progress. Discussing the music and communicating our understandings, as described by Burt-Perkins and Mills (2008, 30–31), played an important role in our process, but for us this focused primarily on technical matters and less on the characteristics of the music. Each person in the trio seemed to carry equal importance; each led the rehearsals at various points. We also employed "dyad practice" (Wulf and Mornell 2008, 8–11), learning through observing one or two of us playing while the other(s) observed, evaluated, or subsequently imitated. At the final rehearsal, before recording, we played the whole Piano Trio as if for a concert, creating performance-like conditions by video-recording ourselves (Barry and Hallam 2005, 157).

There is no question that playing in chamber groups is mimetic in nature. However, I am not convinced that the secret of performing chamber music lies either in finding the right balance between the instruments, as in Kokotsaki (2007, 656–663), or in finding a similar way of playing, as expressed by Lehmann, Sloboda, and Woody (2007, 176–177). Both of these studies describe what musicians would like to achieve, but not how it is achieved. My goal, in slight contrast to these approaches, was to integrate the piano sound as closely as possible with the strings by imagining that these instruments of very different nature could produce a united sound. In doing so, I did not think about how to manipulate my fingers or the pedals, but simply followed and anticipated the sound emanating from my fellows; this is a form of aural communication, predicated upon my embodied understanding of the production of piano sound gained through many years of training and experience (Goodman 2002, 156–158). This links to Juslin and Persson's observations (2002, 224) on the form of communication in which one imagines oneself in the emotional condition produced by the particular experience of united sound, and just lets the music 'happen.' Additionally, although there are considerable differences in the physical movements required for playing string instruments compared to piano playing, analysis of the videos showed that we unconsciously synchronised our body movements at significant musical points.

Interpretation and polystylistic context

Our intellectual decisions with regard to interpretation were connected to the polystylistic contexts of Schnittke's music. Memories of, and associations with, other music from my previous experience determined most of my interpretative choices. The difficulty in performing Schnittke's chamber music lies not just in finding an interpretation, but in creating a musically and technically integrated interpretation. Finding connections between the various tempi of the Piano Trio can be difficult, and this is related to its polystylism. For example, the relationship between the tempi of the first and second movements, *Moderato* and *Adagio*, is informed by the fact that the first theme of the second movement is basically the retrograde of the melody of the first main theme: the tune of "Happy Birthday to You." As a result, in my opinion the *Allegretti* of the first and second movements should be played at the same tempo. Similarly, in the second movement we needed to find a solution with regard to the connection between "*Adagio* (bars 1–8)—a gesture *à la Minuet* (bars 9–15)—*poco più mosso* (bars 16–31)" and "a gesture *à la Minuet* (bars 32–46)—*Adagio* (bars 48–59)." Thus, tempo decisions were often dependent upon contextual factors, rather than being determined solely by the musical factors apparent in any specific phrase or section.

The coded information in Schnittke's score encourages musicians to make choices according to musical background and experience. One striking example, for me, is the second theme of the second movement. On playing this movement for the first time, I recognised that it had a very strong connection to the "Crocodile Gena's Song" from the Soviet cartoon from the 70s, a longstanding Soviet birthday song. However, it was only a few months ago that I finally understood exactly where the allusion lay: in the repetition of the minor second, especially at the beginnings of phrases (as can be seen in examples 3 and 4).

With this realisation, I finally understood the root of the problem I had been experiencing within the chamber group with regard to playing this theme slowly. The association, formed out of my background experience, sent me totally different musical signals compared to my chamber music partners, for whom this phrase had no such associations. Allusions such as this act almost as metaphors, ambiguous in character and dependent "on the performer's personal experience with words and images" (Juslin and Persson 2002, 228)—or, in our case, with music.

Example 3. Alfred Schnittke Piano Trio, movement 2, pages 20–21 (the main tempo of the second movement is Adagio). Alfred Schnittke Trio für Violine, Violoncello und Klavier © Copyright 1992 by Universal Edition A.G., Wien | UE 30163. www.universaledition.com

Example 4. Vladimir Shainsky, "Crocodile Gena's Song" from the animated cartoon *Cheburashka* (the tempo indication is Mobile).

Буратино за фортепиано: попул. дет. песни в самом лег. перелож. — СПб: Композитор, *2004*
[Burattino at the Piano: Easy Arrangements of the Best Known Children's Songs. Sankt-Petersburg: Composer, 2004]

Recording

The two days of recording added little in comparison with the days of rehearsals. There was, however, one great difference: our group had a fourth member, the sound engineer who 'conducted' the course of our recording. We asked his opinion on many aspects of the performance: expressive cues, pitch, ensemble, and the natural flow of the music. On the one hand the sound engineer became an advisor, our 'third ear' outside of the group, and on the other hand we were able to test out our interpretation on him as our first listener.

The first recording of the whole piece (played straight through, as though a concert performance) became our working version of the recording. We listened to the recording, making comments on those sections which were satisfactory and what needed improvement. In contrast to the rehearsals, we talked little and played more. We also practised some short parts that still needed some improvement. Overall, our strategy for the recording process was to avoid obsessive concentration on the micro level of musical perfection, and we alternated between shorter and longer sections. We also recognised that the structure of Schnittke's music is cinematographic in quality (as if a series of separated shots), and this makes it quite suitable for montage-like editing. Perhaps as a result, my partners found that this music was easier to record than to play in a concert hall. Of course, specific to the recording process is the possibility of achieving the desired interpretation synthetically, with short recording takes enabling micro-level concentration on short phrases or even particular tones; at times we recorded certain sections or individual bars with suggestions from the sound engineer for later editing. This is the main difference from the concert situation with its necessarily sustained, macro, level of performing, in which concentration upon each successive individual section, whilst vital, must not overbalance the necessity to keep the whole picture in mind and the music constantly unfolding in real time.

CONCLUSIONS

The musical score provides unlimited possibilities for interpretation. In performing, a musician expresses her or his vision of the form, structure and character of the work through choices of fingering, articulation, rhythmic definition, dynamics, and the use of pedal. Effectively, these choices could be regarded as manifesting the embodied results of the musician's analysis of the score.

In the Western musical tradition, the process of learning is based on the interpretation of score symbols and relates to historical traditions of interpretation. In order to be able to play together, musicians have to interpret these symbols in a similar and co-ordinated fashion. However, Schnittke's polystylistic music challenges musicians in a most unexpected way. The interpretation of his multi-faceted quotations and hidden allusions calls forth particular subjectivities, inseparable from the orientation of each musician's individual historical and cultural background and his or her unique musical memories and associations. Schnittke's polystylistic approach affects the performer not only at the conscious, intellectual level, related to one's explicit interpretative reading of notated instructions in the score, but also at the unconscious, by means of the hidden, associative information embedded in these instructions. Each player absorbs the same information but each reacts differently—the more so because their reaction is at the unconscious level and not explicitly scrutinised or filtered, other than in a more-than-usually reflective process such as the one described here. As Ivashkin writes, "Schnittke's music ... is inseparable from personality—its bright content and delivery need a personal or subjective reading" (Ivashkin 1996, 168–169).

This study has revealed three important findings. First of all, the mapping systems described offer a specific way of working with the score in the process of learning and performing. They exemplify a musician's use of a marking system as a kind of mapping of the piece—although, as indicated, such mapping is almost certainly present even when it operates solely at the internal level. Moreover, the need for two mapping systems (for individual learning and for learning and performing at the chamber music level) reveal changes in the pianist's perceptions. These two mapping systems demonstrate the complexity of the tasks involved in learning and performing chamber music: on the one hand, attention must be paid at an individual level to the comprehensive absorbing and interpreting of the information on the score and, on the other, there is the need to make music together, attending closely to points of ensemble performance and understanding at every moment the constantly changing relationship between one's individual contribution and the whole.

Secondly, the process of individual learning demonstrates parallels with the process of rehearsals, where learning takes place as a group. The micro and macro levels of learning are intrinsic to both processes. The ensemble achieved a harmonisation of tempi, rhythm, phrasing, articulation, dynamics and sound qualities on both the micro level—paying attention to the details of the playing and concentrating on individual, short phrases—and on the macro level—endeavouring to achieve musical continuity and flow, with expressive details internalised or consciously attended to only momentarily. A focus on each level was also evident in the process of recording: the recording situation is somewhat like a performance and, as such, the focus in playing is often on the macro level; but reviewing the playing in the editing process shifts attention to the micro level, with concentration on specific bars or even individual tones.

Thirdly, the drive towards achieving musical affinity plays a central role in the processes of rehearsing and performing of chamber music, and requires a combination of intellectual decision-making and imaginative thinking. Ensemble performance is a multi-levelled activity, demanding highly controlled action and critically reflective thinking, but also intuitive reactions and perceptions, especially in the transformation of the individual into the united sound.

Overall, this investigation has not answered all my questions about the processes of musical learning, but it has, to some extent, exposed and illuminated what can happen behind the 'closed doors' of practice studios, rehearsal rooms and recording studios from a pianist's perspective. Perhaps as importantly for me, the creation of a more-than-usually formal reflective framework around the whole process—from initial, individual, learning through group rehearsal and culminating in a 'final' recording—not only shed light on what was taking place but actually shaped the process itself. In particular, the insights I gained into the ways in which Schnittke's polystylistic references were operating upon me and the other players were deepened and enriched by the systematic regime of reflection through which I approached the whole project.

REFERENCES

Aiello, Rita and Aaron Williamon. 2002. "Memory." In *The Science and Psychology of Music Performance: Creative Strategies for Teaching and Learning*, edited by Richard Parncutt and Garry E. McPherson. Oxford: Oxford University Press, 167–181.

Barry, Nancy and Susan Hallam. 2002. "Practise." In *The Science and Psychology of Music Performance: Creative Strategies for Teaching and Learning*, edited by Richard Parncutt and Garry E. McPherson. Oxford: Oxford University Press, 151–165.

Barry, Nancy. 2000. "Behind closed doors: What really goes on in the practice room?" Paper presented at the meeting of the Southern Chapter of the College Music Society, Lafayette, LA.

Burt-Perkins, Rosie and Janet Mills. 2008. "The role of chamber music in learning to perform: A case study." *Music Performance Research* 2: 26–35.

Buzan, Tony. 2001. *The Power of Creative Intelligence*. London: HarperCollins.

Chaffin, Roger and Gabriela Imreh. 2002. "Practising perfection: Piano performance as expert memory." *Psychological Science* 13 (4): 342–349.

Clarke, Eric, Richard Parncutt, Matti Raekallio, and John Sloboda. 1997. "Talking fingers: An interview study of pianists' views of fingering." *Musicae Scientiae* 1 (1): 87–107.

Clarke, Eric. 2002. "Understanding the psychology of performance." In *Musical Performance: A Guide to Understanding*, edited by John Rink. Cambridge: Cambridge University Press, 59–72.

Deleuze, Gilles and Felix Guattari. 1977. *Rhizom*, trans. Clemens Haerle et al. Berlin: Meuve.

Friberg, Andreas and Giovanni Umberto Battel. 2002. "Structural communication." In *The Science and Psychology of Music Performance*, edited by Richard Parncutt and Garry E. McPherson. Oxford: Oxford University Press, 199–217.

Gieseking, Walter and Karl Leimer. 1972. *Piano Technique*. New York: Dover.

Goodman, Elaine. 2002. "Ensemble performance." In *Musical Performance: A Guide to Understanding*, edited by John Rink. Cambridge: Cambridge University Press, 153–167.

Hallam, Susan. 1995. "Professional musicians' approaches to the learning and interpretation of music." *Psychology of Music* 23: 111–128.

Hultberg, Cecilia. 2002. "Approaches to music notation: The printed score as a mediator of meaning in Western tonal tradition." *Music Education Research* 4 (2): 185–197.

Hultberg, Cecilia. 2008. "Instrumental students' strategies for finding interpretations: Complexity and individual variety." *Psychology of Music* 36 (1): 7–23.

Ivashkin, Alexander. 1994. *Besedy s Alfredom Schnittke* [*Conversations with Alfred Schnittke*]. Moscow: Moscow Culture.

Ivashkin, Alexander. 1996. *Alfred Schnittke*. London: Phaidon.

Ivashkin, Alexander. 2002. *A Schnittke Reader*. Indiana: Indiana University Press.

Juslin, Patrik N. and Roland S. Persson. 2002. "Emotional communication." In *The Science and Psychology of Music Performance*, edited by Richard Parncutt and Garry E. McPherson. Oxford: Oxford University Press, 219–225.

Kokotsaki, Dimitra. 2007. "Understanding the ensemble pianist: A theoretical framework." *Psychology of Music* 35: 641–668.

Krampe, Th. Ralf and K. Anders Ericsson. 1995. "Deliberate practice and elite musical performance." In *The Practice of Performance: Studies in Musical Interpretation*, edited by John Rink. Cambridge: Cambridge University Press, 84–104.

Lehmann, Andreas C., John A. Sloboda, and Robert H. Woody. 2007. *Psychology for Musicians: Understanding and Acquiring the Skills*. Oxford: Oxford University Press.

McPherson, Gary E. and Alf Gabrielsson. 2002. "From sound to sign." In *The Science and Psychology of Music Performance*, edited by Richard Parncutt and Garry E. McPherson. Oxford: Oxford University Press, 99–115.

Miklaszewski, Kacper. 1989. "A case study of a pianist preparing a musical performance." *Psychology of Music* (17): 95–109.

Milstein, Jacob. 1961. "Ispolnitelskie i pedagogicheskie prinsypy K. N. Igumnova" ["Interpretive and Pedagogical Principals of K. N. Igumnov"]. In *Mastera sovetskoj pianisticheskoj shkoly* [*Masters of the Soviet Piano School*]. Moscow: Gosudarstvenoe musykalnoe izdatelstvo, 40–114.

Neuhaus, Heinrich. 1994. *The Art of Piano Playing*. London: Kahn and Averill.

Palmer, Caroline. 1998. "Mapping musical thought to musical performance." *Journal of Experimental Psychology: Human Perception and Performance* 15 (12): 331–346.

Parncutt, Richard and Malcolm Troup. 2002. "Piano." In *The Science and Psychology of Music Performance: Creative Strategies for Teaching and Learning*, edited by Richard Parncutt and Garry E. McPherson. Oxford: Oxford University Press, 285–302.

Parncutt, Richard. 2007. "Can research help artists? Music performance research for music students." *Music Performance Research* 1: 13–50.

Reid, Stefan. 2002. "Preparing for performance." In *Musical Performance: A Guide to Understanding*. Cambridge: Cambridge University Press, 102–112.

Rosen, Charles. 2002. *Piano Notes*. London: Penguin.

Shulgin, Dmitry. 1993. *Godi neizvestnosti Alfreda Schnittke* [*Alfred Schnittke's Years in Obscurity*]. Moscow: Delovaya Kniga.

Wicinski, A. V. 2003. *Process raboty pianista-ispolnitela nad muzykalnym proizvedeniem. Psihologiceski analiz* [*The Pianist-Performer Process of Work on a Musical Composition. A Psychological Analysis*]. Moscow: Klassika XXI.

Wulf, Gabrielle and Adina Mornell. 2008. "Insights about practice from the perspective of motor learning: A review." *Music Performance Research* 2: 1–25.

PERSONALIA

TÂNIA LISBOA is widely acknowledged as one of Brazil's foremost musical personalities with an international profile and an extensive range of recordings. She has performed in Japan, Korea, Turkey, Poland, France, Italy, Spain, Germany, Mexico, Canada, South America and the U.S.A. In addition to standard repertoire, she has recorded the complete works for cello and piano and all the piano trios of Villa Lobos. In her latest CD *The Brazilian Cello,* she champions the equally fine works of lesser known Brazilian composers. Dr Lisboa is currently a Research Fellow at the Royal College of Music in London and a Senior Research Fellow at the Orpheus Institute, Belgium. Her current research focuses on the investigation of musical development, memorizing and practice strategies. She publishes extensively and she is a regular contributor to international conferences, giving papers on performance, music psychology, and music education.

ROGER CHAFFIN is Professor of Psychology at the University of Connecticut where he studies the cognitive processes involved in musical performance. He has reported this research in journals such as *Psychological Science, Music Perception*, and *Music Psychology* and in the book, *Practicing Perfection: Memory and piano performance* (with Gabriela Imreh and Mary Crawford, 2002).

His work on musical memory complements his earlier work on memory and language reported in numerous articles in journals such as the *Journal of Experimental Psychology: Learning, Memory, and Cognition, Cognitive Science*, and *Psychological Bulletin*. He is co-editor of *Memory in Historical Perspective* (1988) and co-author of *Cognitive and Psychometric Analysis of Analogical Problem Solving* (1991). He is a chorister and amateur flautist who has performed solo in public exactly once and prefers running whitewater rapids in a kayak to the excitement of the concert stage.

TOPHER LOGAN is the Director of the Community School of the Arts and a PhD student in the Perception, Action and Cognition program at the University of Connecticut. He is involved in graduate research in the psychology of music with research interests including memory and performance; expressive timing; coordination; and jazz improvisation.

ALESSANDRO CERVINO graduated in piano with honours at the Conservatories of Milan and Brussels and at the Queen Elisabeth College of Music (Belgium). Active as concert pianist, he recently appeared at such important venues and festivals as the Ravello International Piano Festival (Italy), Conservatorio della Svizzera Italiana (Lugano, Switzerland), Centro de cultura musical (Porto, Portugal), Festival of Flanders, and the Musical Instruments Museum and Flagey (Brussels, Belgium). He has recorded a live solo recital for Radio Télévision Belge Francophone and performed various piano concertos with the Flemish Radio Orchestra, the Milano Classica Orchestra, the Sturm und Klang Orchestra, and the Baylor Chamber Orchestra, working with many conductors, including Massimiliano Caldi, Pierre Bartholomée, Thomas Van Haepperen and Stephen Heyde.

Cervino is currently piano professor at the Lemmensinstituut (College of Music & Performing Arts, Leuven), a doctoral student in the performing arts at the University of Leuven within the docARTES programme, and an artistic researcher at the Orpheus Research Centre in Music, Ghent.

CATHERINE LAWS is a musicologist and a pianist specialising in contemporary music. She is a Lecturer in Music at the University of York and a Senior Research Fellow at the Orpheus Institute, Ghent. Her current practice-led research focuses on processes of composer-performer collaboration, and the relationship between physical and sonic gesture. Her musicological research examines the relationship between music, language and meaning, especially with respect to the work of Samuel Beckett and composers' responses to his texts.

Recent publications include: 'On Listening', a guest-edited volume of the journal *Performance Research*; 'Feldman – Beckett – Johns: Patterning, Memory and Subjectivity' in Björn Heile (ed.), *The Modernist Legacy: Essays on New Music*; and 'Beckett and Unheard Sound' in Daniela Caselli (ed.), *Beckett and Nothing*. Forthcoming publications include '"I could show you all I know": Elements of co-creativity in a music theatre context', in *Productive Tensions: Co-creative Practices in Music* (joint edited with William Brooks): this is a further volume of the Collected Writings of the Orpheus Institute. She is also completing a book on Beckett and music for Rodopi Press.

MARIA LETTBERG is an internationally acclaimed concert pianist. She studied piano at the St. Petersburg Conservatoire and the Royal College of Music, Stockholm. The most important milestone of Maria Lettberg's artistic career to date has been the recording of the complete solo piano works of Alexander Scriabin (8 CDs plus DVD). The recordings, which received outstanding reviews, are the result of a period of intensive exploration of the composer's music. Subsequently, she was awarded a doctoral degree on this subject from the Sibelius Academy, Finland, under the guidance of Professor Matti Raekallio. Maria Lettberg's concerts and recordings are complementary with her experience in the field of comparative pianistic analysis of recordings. Her most recent work comprises practice-based research into aspects of creativity in the context of the chamber ensemble, examining artistic processes from the 'inside'. For 2008-2009 Lettberg was a Research Fellow at the Orpheus Research Centre in Music (ORCiM), Ghent. Recently, she has acted as a guest lecturer at the Royal College of Music, Stockholm.

COLOPHON

Editor
Catherine Laws

Authors
Alessandro Cervino
Roger Chaffin
Catherine Laws (ed.)
Maria Lettberg
Tânia Lisboa
Topher Logan

Series editor
William Brooks

Lay-out
Cover: Friedemann Vervoort
naar een ontwerp van Quatre Mains, Maldegem-Donk
Typesetting: Friedemann Vervoort

ISBN 978 90 5867 848 5
D/2011/1869/42
NUR: 664

© 2011 by Leuven University Press – Universitaire Pers Leuven – Presses Universitaires de Louvain.
Minderbroedersstraat 4 – B-3000 Leuven (Belgium).

All rights reserved.
Except in those cases expressly determined by law,
no part of this publication may be reproduced,
saved in automated data files or made public in any way whatsoever
without the express prior written consent of the publishers.